AF351435

Andrea Slingsby

THE DISCIPLINE DIVIDEND

The Leadership Edge
That AI Cannot Replace

Copyright © 2026 by Andrea Slingsby

All rights reserved. No part of this publication may be reproduced or transmitted in any form without prior written permission of the author, except for brief quotations in reviews.

This book is intended for informational purposes only and reflects the author's experience and opinions.

ISBN (Kindle):   978-1-7646852-0-7
ISBN (Paperback): 978-1-7646852-1-4
ISBN (Hardcover): 978-1-7646852-2-1

Independently published via Amazon KDP

First Edition: 2026
Author based in Australia

CONTENTS

DEDICATION:

For my incredible mum, and for my family,
who taught me that showing up, especially when it's really hard,
is where discipline and accountability begin.

FOREWORD

by Graham "Skroo" Turner

I'll be upfront and honest about this book. When Andrea asked me to write the foreword, my first instinct was to tell her it would be a lot more interesting if she just named names in her stories and examples even if she made a few enemies-particularly in Flight Centre-by doing so.

I still think that and maybe that's another book.

But she explained her reasons and seems keen to avoid defamation court cases. She didn't take my word that we would not sue her.

However, I've known Andrea long enough to know that when she's really made up her mind about something, you're wasting your time arguing. That, as it turns out, is rather the point of this book.

For the record (and I suspect many of you have already worked it out) a fair chunk of the "anonymous" leadership experiences in these pages are drawn from a business that I started with a few blokes, a couple of double-decker buses in London, and a beer at Oktoberfest in 1973. This was Top Deck Travel. We then founded Flight Centre in 1982 and built it into something reasonably large. We got a lot of things right. We also got a lot of things spectacularly wrong at various stages. If you've read any part of the book so far, you've probably encountered both.

Andrea joined us when Flight Centre was a fairly small operation of 100 or so Flight Centre Travel Shops but scaling very fast and she joined my global team as we expanded rapidly overseas into New Zealand, the UK, USA, South Africa and Canada.

What struck me about her then, and still does, is that she paid attention to ***why*** things worked, not just ***that*** they worked. Most people in a business just execute and move onto the next thing. Andrea always wanted to understand the system underneath so she could build strong foundations and scale more successfully. That's a different kind of person, and it's a rarer one than you'd think.

I've read quite a few business books in my time. Most of them are written by people who have observed business from the outside, dressed up a few common-sense ideas in language no one actually uses, and charged you fifty dollars for the privilege. This one is different. The discipline, accountability and consistency that Andrea writes about isn't a theory. It's the thing that actually separated the teams that flew in Flight Centre from the ones that floundered. I watched it happen in real time, in our shops, across our business, across multiple countries and all types of economic crises.

We used to say at Flight Centre: *everyone does their own sh*t work*. No one was exempt from the basics. Not me, not the most senior leader in the room. The discipline and accountability wasn't a punishment, it was the foundation and safety net that gave people the freedom to perform. That's what Andrea is getting at, and she probably articulates it considerably better than I ever have.

So, do I wish she'd named us? Yes. Absolutely. I reckon it would've been much funnier.

But I'll admit: the lessons land just as hard without it.

Read it. Apply it. And if you think you've identified some of the characters in it, well you're probably right.

Graham "Skroo" Turner
Founder and CEO, Flight Centre Travel Group

ABOUT THE AUTHOR

Andrea Slingsby is an experienced executive, board director, and advisor who has spent more than three decades leading complex transformations across multiple industries, countries, and organisational lifecycles. She has held C-suite and CEO roles in ASX-listed and private companies, led major international turnarounds, and both served on and advised boards responsible for navigating strategic, cultural, and governance challenges.

Andrea began her career at the frontline and worked her way through functional leadership, global HR, and operational roles into executive and board positions. Both her professional reputation and expertise were built on taking on difficult assignments where drift, under-performance, and cultural disconnect had quietly become normal, and rebuilding the disciplined architecture and consistency needed to restore performance, confidence, and trust. The stories and frameworks in *The Discipline Dividend* are drawn directly from those lived experiences rather than from theory alone.

Andrea now works with boards, CEOs, and senior leadership teams to strengthen accountability, decision architecture, culture, and capability in an era where AI is exposing whether an organisation's discipline is real or cosmetic. Her advisory work includes operational turnarounds, AI and data governance, leadership development, and the design of practical, commercially grounded operating frameworks that stand up under real pressure.

Andrea has held multiple non-executive director and committee roles, including on ASX-listed company boards, and brings a distinctive combination of commercial acumen, people insight, and governance rigour to the tables she sits at. She is known for her directness and pragmatism, her intolerance of theatre and avoidance, and her commitment to making work less needlessly hard for capable people by fixing the systems and processes around them.

When she is not working with organisations, Andrea is continuing to build the broader Discipline Dividend ecosystem, including advisory offerings, self-paced and cohort-based professional development programs for Executives and Board members, and AI-enabled tools that help leaders apply the book's architecture in their own context.

Discipline isn't a constraint.
It's the only thing standing between this and your strategy.

INTRODUCTION

Most senior leaders reading this book are highly capable, well-intentioned, and genuinely committed to the organisations they lead. And yet at some point in their career, often at the precise moment when the stakes and pressure are highest, they find themselves quietly struggling and unsure in ways they cannot fully identify. Carrying more stress than they should, second-guessing decisions they are more than qualified to make, and operating in systems that have been allowed, through understandable choices, to work against rather than for them.

This book is about why that happens, how to see it clearly when it does, and what it actually takes to build the disciplined architecture that makes it stop.

My intent is simple; I want to help people love their work more by feeling and being more capable. As unhappiness and dissatisfaction proliferate at speed in our workplaces, I want to shine a light on what is actually causing much of that struggle and more importantly, what we can do about it. I want to share tools, frameworks, and hard-won insights that help us all be better at our jobs, take genuine pride in what we do, and find real meaning and fulfilment in our working lives.

I felt compelled to highlight a pattern I have watched across both workplaces globally and our broader society: the gradual erosion of discipline, consistency, and accountability. Three proven, foundational principles that, when present, anchor organisations with stability and confidence, and when absent, make our working lives far harder and more uncertain than they need to be.

By showing how these principles are more important now than ever, and by giving you practical tools to rebuild and sustain them, my hope is that this book helps you and the people around you feel better equipped to be the best you can be, both professionally and personally, in a world that is changing faster than most organisations currently know how to absorb.

What this book Is about

Most senior leaders I have worked with across my career have not been short of intelligence, effort, or good intent. What they are commonly short of is something more subtle and far more expensive to ignore: deliberate, consistent, architectural discipline in how they set expectations, hold the line with consistency under pressure, make decisions, and build culture.

Day-to-day, this translates into organisational drift. Standards soften, accountability becomes a bendable line, and performance relies increasingly on individuals outperforming rather than on systems built to produce reliable results. I have watched extremely capable leaders carry impossible loads in environments like this, often blaming themselves for outcomes that were structurally and systemically rigged against them. I have also watched organisations speak impressively about culture, accountability, and well-being, while the reality their people experience every day is something very different. This book is about closing that gap.

Over time, working across many organisations, industries, and countries, I began to see a consistent and striking counter-pattern. When leaders chose discipline, which is sometimes uncomfortable, and then consistently applied discipline over the easier path of narrative, deference, or convenience, performance did not simply improve in the moment. It compounded impressively. Cultures became clearer and far more energising. Decision-making visibly sharpened and became a valued skill set. People's confidence in themselves and in their organisations grew. The organisational returns accumulated quietly, and then unmistakably.

That compounding effect is what I have come to call, **The Discipline Dividend**.

Over time, I have come to think of this as a three-stage pattern that runs through every chapter of this book: Drift, Discipline, and Dividend. Organisations *drift* when standards soften and accountability bends.

Discipline is the deliberate, architectural work of restoring clarity and holding the line. The *Dividend* is what compounds when they do.

I call this the DDD Framework™ and once you see it, you will find it everywhere.

The Discipline Dividend is the compound return organisations and leaders earn when they build and defend disciplined architecture around expectations, accountability, decision-making, and culture. It rarely looks dramatic in any single week or month. But over years, it is precisely what separates the organisations that are quietly, reliably excellent from those that lurch between crises, restructures, and reinventions that never quite land. Like all compounding, it is invisible in the short term and transformational over time.

The language of a "dividend" is deliberate. A growing body of research on habit formation and self-discipline in leadership shows what I have practically observed: that small, consistently repeated behaviours create durable neural pathways and operating norms, while sporadic "big" efforts rarely stick.

Put more simply: talent produces occasional brilliance, but disciplined habits compound into systems that keep working when the heroic effort of individuals stops or they move on. That is exactly what this book is about.

Every chapter that follows is an exploration of one domain where that dividend is available and where the cost of not claiming it is quietly, steadily, and expensively accumulating.

AI is the new X-ray that will expose whether your discipline is real or cosmetic.

Across Chapters 6, 7, and 12, I explore how AI changes the stakes of accountability, governance, and capability; not by replacing the human work of discipline, but by making its absence impossible to hide. The organisations that treat AI as a forcing function for better discipline will gain a significant competitive edge. Those that hope and pray that AI will solve their structural problems without demanding anything of them are heading for a reckoning.

What this book covers

This book has been written from the heart, from lived experience, and from a deep frustration with how unnecessary much of our struggle at work really is. Across three decades in executive, C-suite, global HR, CEO, and advisory roles, I have seen extraordinary people operating in systems that, through no deliberate design, undermine their best efforts in practice. I have also seen somewhat ordinary organisations become genuinely exceptional once they chose to put disciplined architecture in place and refused to let it erode when life got busy, political, or emotionally uncomfortable.

Each chapter examines one domain where discipline either quietly compounds into a dividend, or quietly erodes into cost and disruption.

The first part of this book is deliberately diagnostic. It names the patterns that quietly erode accountability, judgement, confidence, and culture in organisations over time. But diagnosis is only useful if it ultimately leads to action and a better outcome. The second half of this book turns that diagnosis into practical playbooks and toolboxes that leaders can use to rebuild accountability, strengthen decision-making, and create cultures where discipline becomes a source of clarity, trust, and performance rather than fear.

- Chapters 2–4 highlight where discipline and accountability have broken down in organisations, and how that drift shows up in real people's working lives.
- Chapters 5–8 provide the practical playbooks to rebuild the line; how to have the conversations leaders avoid, reset accountability without landmines, and rebuild trust in systems that have been gamed.
- Chapters 6, 7, 10 and 12 focus on judgement and decision architecture; how disciplined thinking and governance pre-

vent the kind of avoidable failures that intelligent boards still find themselves presiding over.

- Chapters 9 and 11 focus on capability and culture; how to build environments where performance, motivation, and well-being are outcomes of design rather than wishful thinking.
- Throughout, I am explicit about where AI helps and where it does not. AI will increasingly expose whether genuine discipline exists in your organisation. It cannot substitute for the human work of building it.

The thread that ties these chapters together is simple: when discipline is architectural and consistent, you earn a dividend across every part of your organisation. When it is optional or episodic, you pay for that choice in ways that are often invisible until the cost is too large to ignore.

Who this book is for

This book is written for people who carry leadership weight in organisations: CEOs and founders, board directors, C-suite executives, business owners, senior leaders, and the HR and people leaders who sit beside them in the hardest conversations. It is also for ambitious and aspiring leaders who can sense that something in their organisation's architecture is "off," and want both the language and a toolkit to name and help shift it.

More broadly, I hope it resonates with anyone who:

- carries responsibility for decisions that matter,
- wants to perform well in a challenging environment and feel better doing so,
- is tired of navigating complexity alone, and
- wants to embrace the AI era with confidence rather than anxiety.

What unites us is not title or seniority. It is the need to think clearly under pressure and to navigate with integrity through increasingly complex times.

If you are looking for a quick fix, a culture program, or an AI tool that will solve your leadership problems without demanding anything of you, this is definitely not that book.

My personal experience is that the leadership lessons that stick with us are generally the ones which were hard learned.

If you are willing to examine how your own standards, decisions, and daily leadership habits are either compounding into a dividend or quietly eroding it, you will find practical, immediately usable tools here.

How to use this book

You can read this book straight through; I have written it so that each chapter builds on the last. But you can also use it diagnostically.

- If accountability conversations are your known weak point, start with Chapters 5 and 8 and work forwards and backwards from there.
- If your concern is board judgement and decision quality, begin with Chapters 6 and 10.
- If you are wrestling with culture and engagement in the middle of a transformation, Chapters 3, 4, 8, and 11 will be most immediately relevant.

At the end of each chapter you will find a toolbox with practical questions and frameworks you can take straight into your next one-on-one, leadership offsite, board meeting, quiet personal reflection or strategy review. They are designed to help you move from insight to action quickly, because the Discipline Dividend is only ever earned in what you actually **DO** next.

As you read, you may find it useful to keep the simple DDD Framework™ in mind as an orienting lens: where is this organisation drifting? Where has discipline been applied or lost? And where is the dividend, or its absence, most visible?

Those three questions will surface more honest answers than most formal diagnostic processes.

A final word

I have not written this book as a theorist or a consultant observing from the sidelines. I have written it as someone who has carried the weight of multiple failing P&Ls in the aftermath of crisis, who has had to rebuild cultures where truth had been quietly replaced by comforting stories, who has made serious mistakes in judgement and in relationships, and who has learned (sometimes slowly and painfully) how to do better.

If there is an edge I bring, it is not perfection. It is a combination of scar tissue, pattern recognition, a commitment to ongoing learning and an unwavering belief that work does not have to be as hard, confusing, or lonely as many leaders find it.

My hope is simple: that this book gives you both the language and the courage to build the kind of disciplined architecture that earns you, your people, and your organisation the Discipline Dividend you deserve, and that when you close the final chapter, you feel more empowered, more equipped, and more confident in your work than when you opened the first.

Warmest regards,
Andrea

The Discipline Dividend:
looks boring this week,
feels brilliant next year.

WHY WE ARE DISCONNECTING AND STRUGGLING MORE AT WORK

"If you're going through hell, keep going."
—Winston Churchill,
former Prime Minister of the United Kingdom

Why are we struggling when we have never been more "connected" at work?

An Introduction to me

Let me tell you a little about myself.

I have no trendy, self-designated or AI-enhanced "superpowers," no delusions of grandeur fanned by vast swathes of social media followers and "likes." In fact, I suspect I am a lot like most of the people who will pick up this book and, hopefully, read it all the way through.

We all arrive at our careers carrying different backgrounds and life experiences, both personal and professional which are shaped by different training and development, different mentors and peers, and different versions of the world that have left their mark on us in ways we are not always fully aware of. That accumulation is what makes each of us genuinely distinctive. It also means we bring wildly different perspectives, techniques, capabilities, and approaches to the work we do, and it is precisely that diversity of experience that allows us to add real, personalised value in ways that cannot be replicated by an AI framework or a formula.

Like many of you reading this, I have traversed a diverse and sometimes bewildering range of roles across a 30-plus-year portfolio career; as an executive, a CEO, an advisor and consultant, a board director and committee member, a mentor, and at various points a combination of all of those things simultaneously. I started at the very bottom of organisations and worked my way upward through persistence and hard work, with the inevitable slips and missteps along the way, grabbing at opportunities to grow whenever they appeared. Those varied roles took me across many industries and geographies, which gave me the chance to build and refine a toolkit of frameworks and approaches that can typically be applied across a broad range of organisations, regardless of size or sector.

It is a curated, accumulated professional skill set; some acquired intentionally and some acquired rather painfully, that has given me both depth and breadth of hard-won experience. It is one that I am justifiably proud of.

Hand-on-heart and without hesitation: I truly love business and organisational transformation, strategy, growth, operational excellence, and everything that comes with the sustained ability to deliver continually evolving and improving outcomes for organisations and the people who work within them.

I am also, I will admit, a somewhat overly enthusiastic organisational problem solver. The more complex and challenging the issues, the more I enjoy unpacking the layers and addressing the root causes rather than the presenting symptoms. No problems visible on the surface? Do not worry; I suspect there may well be some lurking quietly in the shadows, and I will flush them out quickly so we can work on them together and build stronger foundations for the future.

One of the most useful byproducts of my combined experience is what I would describe as a well-developed sense of organisational intuition. A client once referred to me as a "corporate specialist physician," because I had what they perceived as an innate ability to quickly triage the presenting symptoms, block out the noise, and identify the real root cause of organisational issues rather than just treating the symptom most visible at the surface.

That description stayed with me, because it captures something I genuinely believe: that the true cause of most of the issues we encounter at work is rarely where the symptom presents itself. Like many physical diseases, the origin is typically somewhere else in the organisational body entirely, and finding those co-dependencies and systemic causes is work I find genuinely absorbing. The diversity and span of my career, starting with one of my early professional roles in recruitment, has kept my "bullshit detector" well calibrated over the years, and I have found it to be one of the most reliable tools in the whole toolkit.

The other thing you probably need to know about me (and those last few paragraphs may have already given you a hint) is that I am fundamentally a "what's next?" kind of person. I will put my hand up immediately and own it. I am always looking around the corner, always searching for a better state of execution, never fully satisfied with where we are right now, and I will question and challenge everything; especially, and I mean *especially*, when it is presented to me as settled fact. I just cannot help myself, and over the years I have learned to stop apologising for it, because professionally it has served me extremely well in driving continual improvement.

This shows up consistently in how I work. I celebrate success and the achievement of milestones in a meaningful way, and I believe doing this well is genuinely critical to reinforcing goal-oriented behaviour and a high-performance culture, but I am simultaneously and immediately scanning for the next opportunity to improve. I am always searching for better systems, better processes, better technology solutions, better strategic opportunities, better ways to develop the people around me. My desire to continually learn and grow personally is directly reflected in my leadership and advisory approaches at work, and complacency and laziness are not descriptions I have ever had applied to me. Other words, perhaps, and not always flattering ones, but not those.

Ultimately, no matter what kind of business I have been working in across the past three decades, my own professional satisfaction has only ever come from one thing: seeing organisational fundamentals continually evolve and improve to deliver better outcomes, and seeing the people within those organisations grow and flourish alongside them. That is my happy place.

I recently worked with a highly experienced Chief People Officer at a mid-size technology company. She has held the role for four years. She is liked, respected, and by all external measures, performing well. And yet she arrives at our sessions consistently carrying a specific and familiar weight; the sense that the conversations that most need to happen are not happening, that the standards the organisation says it holds are not the standards it actually enforces, and that she is increasingly unsure whether the gap between those two things is her problem to solve or a structural reality she is simply expected to navigate around. She is not struggling because she lacks capability. She is struggling because the system around her lacks discipline. This book is for her and for every leader who recognises that description.

When it comes to business, I believe in doing things properly and not wallpapering over cracks. This does not mean you cannot move fast: in fact, speed is often essential, but my philosophy has always been that the foundations need to be genuinely solid before you build on them, because organisations that scale on weak foundations that rely solely on people instead of due process and consistency do not flourish; they simply fail at greater altitude.

Why we are disconnecting and struggling more at work

I know that most people do not arrive at work intending to struggle. Throughout my career, I have witnessed firsthand the enthusiasm and genuine excitement that people bring to a new role. Nobody turns up on their first day wanting to be somewhere else; they simply do not turn up at all if that is the case.

And yet, as leaders and as organisations, we manage with remarkable consistency to knock that enthusiasm out of people. Sometimes agonisingly slowly, other times with startling speed, but the pattern is depressingly familiar.

The truth is that the majority of people still care deeply about doing good work. I very much believe they want to make sound decisions. They want to feel capable, confident, respected, and valued for the significant portion of their lives they spend at work. And yet across organisations of every size and sector, many capable professionals and leaders find themselves quietly struggling and gradually disconnecting; carrying complex decisions alone, second-guessing themselves privately while projecting confidence publicly, navigating environments that have become harder to navigate without ever quite being able to name why.

Our conversation in this book begins by naming why these behaviours exist, and why they are more prevalent now than they have ever been before. The shifting DNA of our workplace culture is not a personal failure or a leadership flaw; I believe it is a predictable outcome of how modern work and our external environment have evolved. But understanding it as predictable does not make it acceptable, and that distinction matters enormously. What it does mean is that the path back to engagement and great performance is also predictable, and that is the part I find genuinely energising.

Throughout this book, I will also show you that we have more tools at our fingertips than at any previous point in our careers to address this, including some that are new like AI, and many that have simply been forgotten or allowed to erode. That combination of recovered discipline and new intelligence is, in my experience, one of the most powerful forces available to any leader who chooses to use it.

The world is a mess and this impacts us at work

I will be frank: cumulatively, the last several years have felt harder than any comparable period in the past few decades. Wars, terrorism, pandemics, divisive political narratives, manufacturing and supply chain instability and fear, macro-economic and cost-of-living pressures, the continued rise of mental health challenges, amplified extremist views that make society feel as though it is travelling backwards, social media algorithms running riot to manipulate our thinking and behaviour, and environmental, technological, and geopolitical uncertainty pressing on us from every direction. Just re-reading that sentence is enough to produce a low-level sense of nausea, and it is, quite frankly, a lot to carry into a working week.

It feels, for many people, like a persistent dark cloud of apprehension that follows them from home to the office and back again. I feel it myself at times, and I see it clearly showing up in the organisations and workplaces I engage with every day; a kind of "zombie numbness," or survivor mentality which is exhibited as a subtle withdrawal. A disconnection that is difficult to define precisely, but impossible to miss once you know what you are looking for. It manifests in the way people interact with each other, in their commitment to their employers and in the way that leaders are choosing to lead.

In many cases, I observe a pervading sense of individual hopelessness beginning to infiltrate corporate cultures in subtle ways that are hard to name, but unmistakably present. It shows up in the distorted analytics of culture and engagement surveys, in emerging HR and legal issues, in fractured team dynamics, and in the kind of candid "corridor conversations" that never make it into a management report. And yet, surprisingly few organisations have taken the time to deeply examine the compounding impact of these combined pressures and make meaningful structural changes to how they support and engage their people.

Those interventions that have been implemented have been reactive, often superficial, and very much "one size fits all" in their design. They have served, in many cases, as a duty-of-care band-aid; the deliberately minimum acceptable response to a complex and deepening problem. Work from home mandates, wellness programmes, and mental health days are not insignificant, but they do not address root cause. And in the absence of root cause treatment, the same symptoms keep returning, slightly adapted, slightly louder, and slightly more expensive to manage each time.

Over the next several years, this fundamental piece of corporate refocus; around the changing attributes of our workplace cultures, and how to better support our people in ways that produce genuine win-win outcomes for individuals and organisations alike, is going to become a far more critical factor in organisational strategy. It will require a total rethink of how we attract, retain, lead and develop our people. And a critical part of that reimagining will rely heavily on reinstating the known, tested, values-driven outcomes that most organisations take for granted but rarely pressure-test: ensuring that people feel valued, respected, productive, genuinely heard, and meaningfully connected to the purpose of the organisation they have chosen to work for.

Why the AI era changes how we lead and work

This time last year, I could probably have written everything I knew about AI on a small corner of a drink coaster. From a cold start, getting my head around it was simultaneously terrifying and exhilarating; terrifying because I knew that if I failed to embrace it, I risked becoming irrelevant and effectively extinct, and exhilarating because as a long-time transformation leader, I could see the possibilities and opportunities it presented, both strategically and operationally, at the individual and organisational level.

I was also acutely aware of the widening divide among both my peers and the organisations I work with; a growing gap between the early adopters who had stumbled through their initial discomfort and were beginning to genuinely harness AI's potential, and those who had adopted the head-in-the-sand approach and were quietly hoping the whole thing might become optional. I suspect many of you have observed identical behaviour patterns in the people around you.

After many years in leadership and advisory roles, I know how genuinely tough leadership can be, particularly when you are expected to demonstrate mastery of something before you have had adequate time to learn it properly. Getting your head around current AI tools can feel intimidating and risky, especially for less technology-inclined professionals who carry a legitimate fear that they will expose themselves rather than elevate themselves. Early iterations of AI compounded this understandably; unreliable outputs, confident hallucinations, and a general sense that the technology was not yet trustworthy enough to stake professional credibility on.

After taking my own leap of faith and diving in, I quickly realised what I now believe very firmly: artificial intelligence does not replace human judgement, but it does implicitly and dramatically change our expectations around capability, both our own and everyone else's. Having affordable and reliable access to AI tools makes best-practice knowledge and analytical support available to virtually everyone. It surfaces patterns and inconsistencies in ways that are typically faster and more thorough than any individual could manage alone. It challenges our narratives and assumptions without the social politics that often prevent that challenge from happening in person.

Crucially, it reduces plausible deniability, making it significantly easier to stress-test the outputs being presented to us by our teams, and to honestly interrogate the outputs we are presenting to our leaders. And it removes some of the more menial, administrative, and repetitive components of many roles, which creates both an opportunity and an obligation to add more genuine value in the time that is freed up.

In an AI-enabled world, by default we are all expected to be better informed, faster learners, and more confident and disciplined decision-makers. That expectation only works, however, if people are actively supported to embrace AI in a way that helps them think better and not simply pushed to perform better with less support than ever. Traditional learning and development approaches and leadership techniques are not yet optimally aligned with what AI-enabled delivery actually requires, and that gap is both a risk and an opportunity depending on how consciously organisations choose to address it.

AI drives a new contract at work

As access to intelligence facilitated by AI increases, the implicit contract at work changes for everyone involved in it.

What we have instead is a genuine and rare opportunity to leverage AI across organisations to reinstate what many of us have quietly lost sight of along the way: more disciplined thinking approaches and processes; clearer decision-making frameworks and more accessible, reliable support structures; explicit accountability with consistent and disciplined follow-through; and real, supported learning that happens before performance is required rather than instead of it.

We all know that when people are genuinely supported to think well, they struggle less and perform better. AI makes it possible to build more credible foundations for capability development and to facilitate learning at a speed and scale that was simply not accessible before. Ironically, one of the best tools currently available for learning about AI is AI itself; something I encourage every leader I work with to experience firsthand as early as possible.

From disconnect to confidence

Struggle and disengagement at work are not inevitable, despite our rapidly changing world and our tendency to externalise the reasons for both. They have simply been accumulating gradually, in the absence of our full attention to either the causes or the solutions. This has allowed us, collectively, to sidestep responsibility for them and to accept disconnect as a given feature of modern organisational life rather than as a solvable problem.

I have taken over responsibility for multiple businesses and organisations where the culture was visibly and painfully broken; where people were operating at a superficial and ineffective level, where trust had eroded, and where the basic operating architecture of clear expectations, honest feedback, and consistent accountability had all but disappeared. And in each of those cases, with the right approach and genuine commitment, we rebuilt.

We did not announce a transformation programme or roll out a new values framework with a town hall and a poster. We did the unglamorous, methodical work of rebuilding foundations: one clear expectation, one direct conversation, one followed-through commitment and consistent, well planned communication at a time until we had cultures that were genuinely dynamic, engaging, and high-performing.

What I have learned across thirty years is that the path back to confidence, engagement, and genuine performance is not primarily about resilience programmes, mindset coaching, or AI adoption strategies. It is about discipline; specifically, the architectural discipline of building clear expectations, real accountability, honest feedback, and consistent follow-through into the daily operating fabric of an organisation.

That combination, applied consistently over time, pays what I have come to think of as the Discipline Dividend: compound returns in performance, culture, and organisational confidence that are invisible in the first weeks and genuinely transformational across years. The chapters that follow are about how to build it; chapter by chapter and domain by domain in your own organisation.

When people have credible support, structured opportunities to think and learn before they are required to act publicly, and are surrounded by accountability that clarifies and motivates rather than punishes and constrains, they regain confidence. They rediscover the satisfaction and pride in their work that brought most of them to their careers in the first place. It is genuinely wonderful to witness as a leader, and it is entirely within your reach.

Clarity is the shortest distance between
struggle and confidence.

TOOLBOX — Chapter 1

Flushing out disconnect, struggle, and unsupported judgement at work

These questions are not designed to allocate blame. They are designed to surface where work has quietly become harder than it needs to be, and where the blind spots around disconnect actually live. They are deliberately uncomfortable, because no identification of meaningful issues has ever come from asking only the easy questions. I have used these questions; sometimes openly in workshops, sometimes quietly as a diagnostic framework before entering an engagement, to identify where problems exist and where they are deepest.

A. Questions that highlight where people are disconnected and struggling alone

1. Where in our organisation are people expected to make complex or high-impact decisions without a safe way to cross-check their thinking first?
2. Which decisions carry the greatest weight for people and why?
3. Where do people privately express doubt or anxiety that never surfaces in formal forums?
4. Where does confidence appear performative rather than grounded?
5. Who in our organisation is most relied upon and least supported?

**B. Questions that reveal erosion of satisfaction
and meaning at work**
1.   Where have we noticed a gradual loss of energy, pride, or engagement even among capable performers?
2.   What parts of work feel draining rather than satisfying, and when did that begin?
3.   Where in our organisation do people feel they are "getting through" work rather than growing through it?
4.   How often do we talk about performance outcomes without talking about how the work actually feels?
5.   What signals of disengagement are we normalising because they appear manageable or widespread?
6.   How deeply do we analyse feedback and data from leavers and low performers?

**C. Questions that identify unsupported judgement
and decision pressure**
1.   Where are people expected to be certain before they have had time to learn, reflect, or test assumptions?
2.   Which roles or individuals are carrying disproportionate decision risk or pressure without proportional support?
3.   Where are people relying on instinct alone because structured thinking support is absent?
4.   How often do we press for speed and decisiveness without stress-testing the underlying assumptions?
5.   Where do people fear making the wrong decision more than they fear making no decision at all?

**D. Questions that test whether foundations are being built or
wallpaper is being applied**
1.   Which recurring problems have we "fixed" multiple times over the past five years without addressing their root cause?

2. Where are we treating symptoms rather than strengthening foundational causes?

3. What issues keep re-emerging in slightly different forms?

4. Which systems, processes, or expectations are no longer fit for the current environment but remain untouched?

5. Where have short-term fixes quietly become long-term arrangements?

E. Questions about leadership, support, and the new AI-enabled reality

1. How has our approach to supporting thinking and judgement evolved as work has become more complex?

2. Where are we expecting people to use AI tools without helping them learn how to use them well?

3. What fears or resistance around AI are we ignoring rather than addressing?

4. Where could AI be used to reduce struggle, not just increase output?

5. How are we using new tools to improve capability rather than simply to raise expectations?

F. Questions that reframe discipline as support

1. Where have we avoided clarity in the name of empathy, and what has that cost?

2. Which expectations are implicit rather than explicit?

3. Where would earlier, clearer intervention have reduced uncertainty or stress?

4. Where would better discipline actually make work easier and more satisfying for everyone involved?

Closing reflection — Chapter 1

Struggle, disconnect, and dissatisfaction at work do not appear overnight. They accumulate in the space where complexity increases but clarity, support, and discipline do not keep pace and they tend to become visible only once they have already become expensive. None of this is inevitable, and none of it is beyond your influence as a leader. It is both your job and entirely within your control to be aware of the symptoms, understand the causes, and drive the solutions proactively rather than reactively.

Here is a space for your own reflection on this chapter. What resonated with you?

(Write your thoughts here)

CHAPTER 2

HOW DRIFT AND UNDER-PERFORMANCE BECOME NORMAL

"How did you go bankrupt? Two ways. Gradually, then suddenly."

— Ernest Hemingway,
Nobel Prize-winning Author
The Sun Also Rises, 1926

During my career as both an executive and an advisor, I have frequently encountered organisations where consistent focus and genuine forward motion are the hardest things to sustain. Every day can feel like the proverbial "same sh#t, different day". This is a mantra I hear repeated with weary familiarity in corridors and car parks and behind closed office doors, by people who have long since stopped expecting anything to change. In these organisations, there are almost always urgent "fires" to fight on a daily basis, that consume the majority of available bandwidth in key people, ensuring the deferral of shorter-term objectives, and by default, quietly strangling forward momentum. I will put my hand up immediately and admit that it has happened to me and under my watch, more than once.

Early on in my career, I was overseeing a support division of a large corporate entity where, in the beginning, we genuinely could not tell whether we were actually achieving anything meaningful at all. Day-to-day activities continued, people came to work and went home late having been extremely "busy," but I could tell we were not making a real difference, and it frustrated me enormously. To find a solution, alongside the ongoing demands of business-as-usual, I needed to pull apart what I have come to affectionately describe as "the rugby scrum"; person by person, role by role, position description by position description, KPI by KPI, and strategic alignment element by strategic alignment element, to work out what the best way to rebuild the function actually was, so that we could make a real and meaningful contribution to the company.

I called it the rugby scrum because from the outside it looked like a lot of committed people pushing hard, but from where I was standing it was almost impossible to tell who actually had the ball.

My memory of going through this tedious yet crucial activity was definitely akin to undergoing a root canal.

Knowing we were a very long way from operating optimally, I looked outside first, seeking out external experts and innovators who were thinking about our traditional function in different and more effective ways. We looked at innovation in businesses and industries outside our own, alongside macro trends, to forecast where the opportunities lay for us to contribute more effectively. At the same time, we exhaustively spoke to (and more importantly, listened to) our internal customers and stakeholders to gauge what we currently did well, what we did not, and where and how they felt there were gaps in support and service. Their feedback, in many cases, was absolutely brutal. No-one who takes pride in their work enjoys hearing that the service they thought was merely stretched is, in fact, driving other people quietly mad. But we took it on the chin, because that information was gold when resetting our new operating model and it became our north star when recalibrating and aligning our KPIs and service standards.

I can highly recommend it [this approach] to anyone reading this who is thinking "those symptoms sound a little like our business." A word of warning, though: it is not a "set and forget" activity.

Drift and complacency set in much faster than any of us wish to acknowledge, which is why I have always found regular customer and organisational review and reset to be genuinely essential rather than optional. I typically did this annually, with embedded internal customer satisfaction mechanisms running throughout the year to ensure we remained aligned and delivering the best possible outcomes.

In the following chapters, I will walk you through the details of that major divisional transformation in full. But what really struck me in those very early days, when I knew there was a problem but had not yet worked out the way forward, was that under-performance, disconnect and misalignment rarely announce themselves as a single, definitive failure. More often than not, they embed quietly in the DNA of an organisation through repeated habits, reinforced behaviours both conscious and unconscious, tolerance, poor role definition, inadequate outcome analysis, and through the narratives and stories we repeat to ourselves and each other without ever stopping to question whether they are actually true. What begins as a temporary accommodation: in roles, focus, and deliverables becomes, over time, a stable and accepted operating norm with no clear starting point and no obvious moment at which anyone chose it. In my career, I have consistently called this "drift," and it takes many forms: strategic drift, cultural drift, leadership drift, capability drift, and operational or systemic drift.

In this chapter, I will share my insights and experiences into how intelligent, well-intentioned, and often highly credentialled leaders at the helm of organisations can come to quietly accept outcomes they would once have challenged and why this drift is so difficult to see from the inside without robust frameworks embedded to monitor and identify it.

Not because the warning signs are absent, but because they are hiding in plain sight, so obvious and so familiar that they cease to register with us.

How drift actually embeds inside organisations

Welcome to your annual performance review.
Don't worry, I'm reading your file for the very first time with you.

Drift is not an event; it is a process

Most people who have spent time inside organisations will likely recognise drift instinctively. They may not have named it before, but we have all undoubtedly felt or observed it: that slow recalibration of expectations, that quiet implied acceptance of things that would once have prompted concern and further probing, and the gradual normalisation of outcomes that are, at best, adequate and, at worst, a profound lost opportunity for the organisation.

One of the most common misconceptions I encounter when organisations talk about under-performance is the belief that it arrives at a definable moment in time; a bad quarter, a failed strategy, a competitor shock that suddenly exposes a weakness. In reality, my experience shows that it almost never begins that way. Rarely do boards or executives or leadership teams wake up one morning and consciously decide to lower their standards.

What I have seen repeatedly, across industries and organisational lifecycles, is that drift embeds through a series of individually defensible decisions that accumulate over time. I have personally been the architect of this sequence of small adjustments where no single decision (made often in haste) appears obviously out of kilter. Each seems to makes logical sense in context when viewed through the lens of pressure, complexity, competing priorities, and the genuine "busy-ness" of high-performing environments that we work in. I have found that often it is only with distance or hindsight that the cumulative impact becomes obvious, which is precisely what makes it so challenging to interrupt without deliberate frameworks applied rigorously and regularly.

How reasonable decisions
add up to unreasonable outcomes

Drift almost never starts with someone obviously dropping the ball. In my experience, it usually starts with someone being quite reasonable and accommodating over an extended period of time.

Perhaps we have seen a project or outcome falling short, but the explanation is really quite convincing at the time. The environment (internally or externally) may have genuinely been quite difficult or hard to control. In a fast-moving organisation with a full "to-do" list and a dozen other daily fires often on the go, our natural instinct is to accept the explanation presented to us and move forward. Often because there are more urgent things demanding our attention and let's be honest, nobody wants to be the leader who makes a big deal out of a one-off slight miss (do we!?).

Then something similar happens again and the explanation you get may be slightly different this time, but similar enough to let it slide. Again. There could still be enough positive news stories, and enough noise in the system around us, to make our leadership patience feel like the better decision in that moment.

I worked with one organisation where the monthly results were, almost routinely, "a little behind budget", but always for *very* good reason. And the reasons were often genuinely impressive and comprehensive in their variety and cadence: a system upgrade issue, an unexpected resignation or the well-worn "resourcing issues". While none of them were stand-outs or silly in isolation, the cumulative pattern was hard to ignore and eventually caught up with us in the same way a slap in the face with a wet fish does. Cold and confronting. By the time people around our meeting room table recognised that "for good reasons" had quietly become cultural code for "we are never going to hit this/nor do we really believe we have to," the hard budget targets had effectively become optimistic suggestions.

That is usually how I see drift take hold in our organisations.

Accountability does not often collapse in a single moment in our day but incrementally dissolves in rooms full of smart, well-meaning people who do not yet see what those calls are adding up to collectively. When we neglect to regularly take time out of our diaries to analyse trends and reflect on what's really going on around us, it is remarkably easy for it to set in. The discipline of regular, quiet times of leadership reflection and real data analysis when you choose to only focus on working "on" and not "in" the business, has proven for me to be a great way to counteract the accumulation of incrementally poor decisions.

The shift from managing performance to managing comfort

One of the clearest early signs I see that drift is taking hold is a shift in what our leadership conversations actually focus on. It happens so gradually that most people don't notice it until it is well and truly locked in.

Early in a working relationship, especially when a leader and their direct report are still finding their feet together, conversations tend to be genuinely about performance with lots of clear direction and support. Are you clear on what needs to be done and where we are heading? Do you have everything you need to achieve the right results? What drove that outcome or result? What needs to change and by when? At the start, there is usually a healthy level of curiosity and a reasonable tolerance for direct feedback on both sides of the table.

Then for reasons we rarely stop to examine, we assume those conversations are no longer required and the focus begins to move. Our conversations start to become more about managing and meeting expectations, protecting morale, and keeping momentum. Performance is still technically on the agenda, but often discussed at a higher altitude, with less specificity, less genuine curiosity, and less follow-through on the things that were supposed to have changed since last time. Like most interpersonal relationships, we tend to build up a set of assumptions about the individuals that we are working with (either consciously or subconsciously) and this forms the filter through which our subsequent conversations are framed.

Both sides get better at the politics over time too, which is part of the problem. We all learn (consciously or not) what to say, how to frame things to preserve the relationships, and what is better left unspoken in order to land the most favourable read of the situation. Uncomfortable or honest observations get smoothed over in the name of support and stability.

If, like me, you have ever walked out of a performance conversation thinking, *"We just spent an hour together and somehow concluded that everything is basically fine and nothing needs to change"*, then you have experienced this first-hand. What started as a genuine performance discussion has quietly become a comfort management exercise that "ticks the HR box" without doing any of the meaningful work.

I want to be clear: the core idea of maintaining constructive, productive relationships in high-performing teams is absolutely valid. The danger creeps in when the desire to keep everyone comfortable starts to matter more than being honest, and when harmony quietly outranks clarity. Once the desire for interpersonal comfort sits above candour and transparency, everyone's learning slows, capability stalls, engagement drops, and drift picks up speed in ways that are genuinely hard to unwind.

Most leaders are not avoiding hard conversations because they are lazy or indifferent. They are trying not to create unnecessary anxiety, and in an increasingly litigious environment many are acutely aware of the personal risk if a performance conversation goes sideways. The time, distraction, and emotional toll of formal processes and legal and commercial risk is real. It is a legitimate reason some leaders hesitate to initiate the conversations that might have prevented the problem in the first place.

But when comfort repeatedly outweighs clarity in the conversations that shape performance and culture, the organisation undoubtedly pays for that choice; in trust, in standards, and eventually in results that can no longer be explained away.

I encourage everyone to save the "Zen" for your meditation retreat. Have the respect for your teams to have the difficult and necessary conversations in an honest, transparent, supportive and timely manner. They may not enjoy it in the moment, but they will absolutely trust you more in the long run.

Why capable people rarely interrupt drift early

Drift is rarely driven by people looking the other way on purpose. In my experience, it is usually sustained by capable, experienced people who are genuinely trying to do the right thing, often under intense and competing pressures.

To effectively interrupt organisational drift means actively challenging assumptions and being brave enough to backtrack and revisit decisions everyone thought were fully resolved.

Logically, it feels like something we should all be comfortable doing, but in many workplace cultures that is simply not the reality.

I have personally been the source of a lot of frustration for peers and teams by wanting to revisit crucial decisions they felt were well and truly laid to bed, simply because they did not sit well with me. By not looping back I feared we were building upon weak foundations that would trip us up later.

Sometimes it means asking questions that can feel wildly disproportionate to the issue in front of you that day. It means slowing down at precisely the moment when everything around us is demanding speed and crisp, clean answers. It means being willing and comfortable to sit in short-term tension in service of longer-term clarity and alignment. In busy, fast-moving environments, those behaviours are often quietly deprioritised, and occasionally, if we are honest, actively discouraged.

None of this happens because people stop caring. I see the opposite. It happens because they care *so* much about delivering results on time, because they are committed and loyal, and because the immediate cost of challenge feels sharp, visible, and personal while the cost of drift and "kicking the issue down the road" feels distant and more manageable.

The problem is that it is not manageable. It is simply deferred… with compound interest. Unfortunately, it compounds even when no-one remembers consciously signing up for that particular investment strategy.

How drift becomes invisible from the inside

The hardest thing about drift, I find, is that it rarely shows up as a dramatic moment. There is usually no flashing red light on a dashboard, no single meeting with an "aha!" moment where everyone suddenly "sees the light" of the problem at the same time. Instead, you get a muddle of results that disguise the problem. Some things are going well enough, others are clearly off, and together they create a kind of organisational blur that lets us assume "It is not great, but it is definitely not a crisis either."

Week by week, there are just enough "good news stories" around us to defend what we are already doing, and more than enough "context" to explain away what is not working. All of it sounds perfectly reasonable in isolation.

Meanwhile, through our lack of focus what we are often missing, is that the baseline of expectations has shifted underneath us. Targets and performance that would once have felt embarrassing at the start of the year, get gradually reframed as "pretty good, considering". Cultural behaviours that would previously have triggered a hard conversation or even formal performance management are rationalised. What used to be a clear line in the sand about expectations from management becomes extremely pliable.

From the inside, often nothing seemed to change overnight. From the outside, the same warning signs have often been sitting in reports, meetings, and hallway conversations for months or even years, repeated so often that they stopped sounding like warnings at all. We have all lived our own "Groundhog Day" versions of this reality. A colleague of mine used to describe it, with a wry smile, as "living the dream".

When experience, trust, and past success begin to work against us

One of the reasons drift seems so persistent is that it is often reinforced by the very things organisations and leaders tend to value most: experience, accumulated trust, and past success. On the surface, these are unambiguously positive attributes and ones that we all aspire to. In practice, they can quietly undermine discipline if they are allowed to run unchecked at the precise moment when consistent performance standards start to falter.

I have worked with many leadership teams and boards who are genuinely capable, well-intentioned, and deeply invested in the success of their organisations. These are not careless or incompetent people. In fact, they are highly credentialled, highly experienced, and highly committed. And yet, over time, I have watched drift take hold in environments that, on the face of it, appeared well protected from it.

The pattern I see is depressingly familiar. Leaders who have delivered strong results in the past, and through that have made their leaders and their organisations look good, are consciously or subconsciously extended greater latitude over time. Their judgement is trusted, sometimes implicitly. Their decisions are questioned less and less rigorously, not because anyone is asleep at the wheel, but because challenging them starts to feel futile and carries more risk than potential reward. At times, I have personally feared it would be seen as disloyal to actively ask difficult questions given the goodwill that had been accumulated over time. Our organisations tend to remember what worked before, and that memory imprints in the cultural DNA, carrying disproportionate weight in how we behave.

Initially, this trust is earned and entirely appropriate. The difficulty arises when trust starts to substitute for scrutiny, when implied competence replaces demonstrated and current evidence of it, and when the benefit of the doubt quietly becomes a standing policy rather than a case-by-case assessment.

Professor Frances Frei from Harvard Business School, author of the excellent business book *Unleashed*, describes what she calls the "Trust Triangle": three essential pillars of authenticity, logic, and empathy that together form the foundation for building, maintaining, and rebuilding trust in individuals and organisations. We all operate on the understanding that boards must trust their CEOs, executives must trust their teams, and peers must trust each other for organisations to function effectively and productively. But trust has a shadow side, and we rarely recognise it until something goes dramatically wrong and the drift suddenly becomes unmissable.

When implied trust becomes a substitute for scrutiny and accountability, discipline erodes – and it does so without anyone noticing, which is precisely what makes it so corrosive. Over time, familiar leadership relationships, often deepened by genuine personal connection built across years of shared experience, can create assumptions of competence that feel too uncomfortable to question, a benefit of the doubt bias because someone seems to know what they are talking about and has delivered decent results in the past, a reluctance to probe deeply out of fear of being perceived as micromanaging, and a general discomfort challenging known and respected figures who might make you look foolish in the process.

I have lost count of the number of times I have seen these dynamics play out in boardrooms and senior leadership forums across industries, where "performance explanations" are accepted, reframed, and celebrated without interrogation, while failure is contextualised through expert narration rather than examined with genuine intent to learn. This is how trust bias forms. Once it is embedded, it quietly and often quite dramatically reshapes governance and leadership behaviour in ways that no one would have consciously chosen, and that most of us would be deeply uncomfortable to acknowledge.

When familiarity reduces curiosity and scrutiny

The boards and leadership teams most susceptible to drift are often those who have worked together the longest. I believe that long tenure is not in itself a problem, however the natural deepening of relationships that occurs over time carries an inherent and often unacknowledged risk. People learn each other's styles, preferences, and pressure points. Meetings flow with less friction. There is less need to explain context or revisit history. The congeniality is productive and genuine in many respects, but it is also where assumptions go untested, because "we've seen this before." Explanations are accepted quickly because they sound plausible coming from a trusted voice. Decisions move through forums with little resistance, not because they are always sound, but because challenging them feels unnecessary or uncomfortable.

What frequently goes unnoticed is that the external environment has changed, even when the people in the room have not. At that point, past experience begins to substitute for current evidence, and the organisation shifts from learning forward to relying backward on well-worn and largely untested narratives.

This is not arrogance. It is simply established human interpersonal relationships beginning to profoundly influence and quietly dilute the quality of organisational decision-making.

The quiet protection of sacred cows

Everyone knows Gerald. Nobody mentions Gerald.
Gerald has been here for twelve years.

Every organisation I have worked in or around has a Gerald. The name changes, the job title and divisional paddock they graze in changes, but the organisational choreography around Gerald is remarkably consistent. Another dynamic I see repeatedly is what I call the preservation of "sacred cows" – the individuals, roles, functions, or long-standing strategies that are no longer questioned in the same way everything else is, protected by history, relationships, or an implied indispensability that is rarely tested with rigour. I have sat in countless meetings where everyone in the room could see the issue clearly, yet no one was prepared to name it.

The rest of the organisation typically sees it even more clearly, and they draw their own conclusions about what is really valued and what the true standards of accountability actually are.

Every time an exception is made for the sake of harmony, the disconnect and drift is reinforced. My own experience with sacred cows of the two-legged variety who were on our payroll is that no matter how indispensable they appear to be, a quick process and quantifiable impact filter applied to their actual contribution often reveals a reality that falls far short of the implied value. I twice made the mistake of leaving this impact unchecked and unvalidated for far too long, allowing people to remain in roles past the point at which they could contribute productively in a measurable way.

In both cases, the qualitative feedback and palpable relief from the rest of the organisation after they eventually left was revealing and validating, and a reminder that the cost of tolerance is always higher than it appears in the moment.

The uncomfortable truth was that the team understandably thought less of my own leadership by letting those people remain in their roles for far too long. The damage extended far beyond the impact of the individual themselves.

Why governance often fails to interrupt drift

Governance is supposed to act as a counterbalance to organisational drift. In theory, boards, committees, and governance frameworks exist to ensure strategic alignment, challenge assumptions, test decision quality, and ensure that standards remain clear as internal and external complexity increases. In practice, no matter how well-credentialled the individuals involved, governance frequently struggles to fulfil this role effectively. I have worked with boards that are conscientious, engaged, and well-meaning, and yet still fall into patterns that allow drift to continue; patterns that become self-reinforcing precisely because they do not feel problematic while they are forming.

Board reports are thorough and lengthy, sometimes distractingly so, but discussion around underlying trends is often shallow as time and attention veer toward the latest strategic priority, the "bright and shiny" objective or the packed Board meeting agenda. I have found that board agendas, like wardrobes, have a habit of becoming crowded with things that once seemed essential and now simply make it harder to find what matters. Issues are sometimes noted and parked rather than explored and fully resolved. Trends are tracked but not linked to clear minimum accepted levels with explicit intervention mechanisms attached.

Over time, as this pattern repeats, governance shifts subtly from intervention to observation. This is typically the result of competing pressures, limited time, and a genuine desire to be supportive rather than obstructive. But when governance becomes primarily about reassurance and harmony rather than constructive challenge, its ability to interrupt drift diminishes rapidly, and drift no longer meets the resistance it requires.

The emotional cost of naming the problem

One of the most significant reasons drift is so hard to challenge is that doing so requires confronting a set of deeply uncomfortable truths and implementing new ways of working across multiple levels of the organisation simultaneously. It requires acknowledging that past decisions may not have had the impact intended which is rarely easy, especially for people whose professional identity is closely linked to their track record of getting things right. It requires revisiting assumptions that have become familiar and therefore effectively invisible.

Most importantly, it requires recognising that well-intentioned behaviours – in particular protecting people, maintaining stability and avoiding conflict – may have been actively contributing to the very problems the organisation is experiencing. For leaders and boards, this can feel deeply personal, and for many, the impulse to maintain the outward perception of competence and integrity makes the honest acknowledgement of drift feel professionally threatening in a way that is difficult to overstate.

Why drift feels personal before it looks organisational

One of the most insidious qualities of drift is the way it shows up for individuals long before it is acknowledged at an organisational level. We can often observe that very capable people begin to feel generally uneasy and increasingly frustrated. Noticing decisions that do not quite add up, they sense that standards are shifting without being able to point to a single moment or policy change that explains the feeling, and they carry the weight of increasing responsibility alongside declining clarity and support.

Because the organisation continues to function around them, these individuals often mistakenly assume that the problem lies with them. They tend to question their own judgement and then often they work harder to compensate. They carry uncertainty privately while projecting confidence publicly. Over time, this creates exactly the kind of struggle described in the previous chapter even among people who are, by any objective measure, performing well.

This is why drift is so deeply damaging at the individual level. By the time it becomes visible in performance metrics, it has often already taken a significant toll on the confidence, energy, and sense of purpose of some of the organisation's best people. And it leads, with uncomfortable regularity, to capable and valuable individuals self-selecting themselves out of the organisation.

I am consistently struck by the lack of genuine, robust inquiry into the circumstances that led to the departure of strong performers. Time pressure and the urgency of filling the vacant role too frequently take precedence over the far more valuable question of what organisational or leadership patterns contributed to the loss. A poor recruitment choice, a leadership failure with a pattern of high turnover, systemic gaps in induction or feedback or clear communication and clarity of objectives and performance expectations; all of these are identifiable and improvable, but only if we are willing to examine them honestly, without ego, and with a genuine commitment to doing better the next time.

How language softens without anyone noticing

One of the earliest and most reliable signals of drift I have observed is a subtle change in the language commonly used across the business, particularly at the leadership and executive level. Goals and targets that were once described as "missed" or unacceptable become "in line with or better than market conditions/competitors." Performance that would previously have triggered concern is reframed as "mixed" and not deemed worthy of deeper analysis. Risks are acknowledged, but almost always accompanied by reasons why they are acceptable, temporary, or already well managed.

None of these phrases are necessarily wrong in isolation, in fact most are technically accurate, and context genuinely matters. What changes however is the cumulative effect.

As language and clarity soften, urgency dissipates, and precision is often lost. Conversations feel calmer, but also less useful. Over time, people stop pushing for clarity because the narrative feels settled and comfortable, and because the cost of challenging it no longer seems proportionate to the return. This is one of the most effective ways drift hides in plain sight, wearing the respectable mask of measured and considered communication.

Metrics and reporting: why standing on the scales doesn't drop the weight

I have yet to meet anyone who lost weight by admiring the bathroom scales, and yet organisations do the performance equivalent of this every month.

Most organisations I work with have no shortage of data. In fact, most have an overabundance in the form of dashboards produced regularly, reports detailed and consistent, performance metrics tracked diligently. From the outside, this creates the appearance of everything being firmly under control. Inside the organisation, however, a very different pattern often emerges: the same reports appear month after month, the same figures are discussed, the same explanations are offered, and very little actually changes.

In the worst case scenario (which is far more common than you may expect) reports get published that absolutely no-one within the organisation reads, responds to or uses to frame actions.

I have sat in countless meetings where performance reports are presented, noted, and accepted with minimal interrogation or genuine curiosity. There may be questions asked at a surface level, issues acknowledged but rarely pursued to resolution, and the data ultimately confirming what people already expected to see and therefore no longer prompting curiosity or challenge.

At that point, make no mistake; measurement has completely lost its power. It is no longer a tool for learning or correction but has become the corporate equivalent of a comfort object. The "standing on the scales" problem is a real one in my experience. When the act of measuring is confused with the ***discipline of acting*** on what the measurement is telling you, and when those two things come apart, reporting practically become a shield to accountability rather than a window into performance.

A personal case study:

How accountability improves with process and structure
Accountability is firmly embedded in my DNA as a practitioner, and it has formed the backbone of every organisational design project I have ever contributed to. My own understanding of what genuinely effective accountability looks and feels like was forged early in my career, in a high-growth business where discipline and accountability were not only highly valued but extraordinarily well executed.

The business measured everything that mattered: across all divisions, both front-facing and back-end support functions including marketing, HR, technology, and beyond. Their core philosophy, applied with disciplined consistency throughout, was simple: "what gets measured and rewarded, gets done."

From that foundation, I set about transforming the global HR function I was responsible for, developing a fully integrated performance accountability model for HR that was later featured in national publications and presented at universities and industry events. In its mature state, the model included clearly defined specialised functional responsibilities modelled on external best-practice businesses and treated as true profit centres. Service level agreements provided fee guarantees and refund mechanisms modelled on external competitors, and clear profitability goals that reflected genuine value to the organisation. Every individual within those HR businesses had balanced scorecard KPIs aligned to broader organisational objectives, measurable at an individual rather than a team level. Every single month, a HR KPI handbook was published to the whole business showing how *every HR professional in every division* was performing against those agreed KPIs, ranked from top to bottom and with aligned recognition and rewards for top performers.

Unsurprisingly, it was not universally loved on day one. Transparency rarely is. But the benefits to the majority outweighed the initial discomfort of the minority and those who didn't feel comfortable operating in that environment self-selected.

The results were transformative in ways that, in hindsight, should perhaps not have been surprising but felt genuinely remarkable. Productivity and delivery outcomes improved not by modest increments but meteorically.

The results were significant. Recruitment times fell from a twelve-week global average to under two weeks. Staff turnover dropped, new hire performance in the first twelve months improved materially, and the teams themselves thrived on the recognition and the professional transparency the model gave them. Over four years, we achieved Best Employer recognition across four countries including, later, in the North American transformation described in Chapter 9, where we maintained that recognition despite operating through one of the most significant commercial disruptions in the company's history.

What I learned was not primarily about HR metrics. It was about the compound effect of designing a system where measurement, accountability, recognition, and development were integrated rather than sequential, and where the discipline of maintaining that integration, especially when it was inconvenient, was precisely what produced the returns.

I learned that the secret ingredient was the full and complete integration of every aspect of the model applied simultaneously and in optimal alignment with each other. Implementing individual elements in isolation never produces the same outcomes, because the co-dependencies between those elements are precisely where the power resides. The model worked like an onion with many interdependent layers: great processes and control mechanisms, a balanced approach to measurement with genuine quality and productivity outcomes, full transparency of results, aligned reward and recognition, and credible professional development all working seamlessly together to motivate, engage, lift capability, and optimise outcomes in a self-reinforcing cycle.

I remain immensely proud of what we achieved as a team during that major transformation and am profoundly grateful for the lessons it taught me about discipline, accountability, process design, and the genuine power of alignment.

But we couldn't do that here

Across my advisory career, I have found that very few organisations enforce performance and accountability with anything approaching that level of rigour. In fact, I typically find quite the opposite: disjointed and often poorly designed KPI sets, misaligned incentives that get tweaked without any real understanding of the flow-on implications, a strong reluctance to critically examine existing accountability frameworks, and well-worn narratives about why a more disciplined approach would not work here; particularly in support functions, which often seem to occupy an almost untouchable status.

The reluctance of support functions like finance, HR, technology and marketing to embrace and enforce the same level of *individual* productivity and accountability rigour and focus that the revenue producing areas of the company are exposed to has constantly puzzled and surprised me. Quite simply, the opportunity for improvement presented by the alignment and combination of the two seems obvious on its face and I have seen this in practice myself.

Over time, I have observed consistently that metrics and performance lose their edge when they are reported but not genuinely interrogated, when exceptions and excuses become routine, when targets are revised and KPIs manipulated without transparency or consequence, and when explanations are accepted without independent verification.

Measurement without integrity, aligned processes, and genuine consequence does not drive performance; it just creates noise and activity that consumes energy and resources without producing meaningful change. Eventually, poorly designed or inconsistently applied dashboards become more comfort objects than accountability tools, which sends a strong smoke signal from the top that "we are watching." In fact, the absence of robust interrogation or intervention communicates the far more powerful message that the watching will never lead to anything.

When reporting becomes a shield

As organisations grow, reporting inevitably becomes more layered. Information is summarised, aggregated, and filtered as it moves upward through the structure; context is added, but meaningful analysis and honest commentary are often absent. By the time information reaches senior leadership or the board, much of its original texture has been carefully smoothed out at multiple levels to remove anything potentially offensive. Most often, the result is that the quality of the narrative is often generic, professionally presented, and almost entirely devoid of the friction that genuine transparency would produce.

I have reviewed board papers that run to hundreds (even thousands) of pages and that communicate, with consummate professionalism and palatable tone, precisely nothing that is clearly uncomfortable or unresolved.

There are few things more impressive, or more dangerous, than a beautifully formatted document that avoids the only question that matters.

I have also experienced the equally effective alternative strategy of bombarding recipients with micro-level detail so overwhelming that those reading are left too exhausted to ask any-thing meaningful and quietly grateful to move on to the next agenda item. Neither approach is typically malicious; both are a function of scale, structure, and the deeply human instinct to present work in the most favourable light. But the risk arises when those receiving the reports stop asking what they are *not* seeing, and when those producing them stop being genuinely motivated to illuminate what is not working as clearly as what is.

When that happens, reporting becomes a shield to true accountability rather than a window, and drift accelerates because it is no longer being directly confronted.

Why process starts to substitute for progress

Another pattern I see with striking regularity is the quiet elevation of process over progress, specifically the organisational tendency to reassure itself that because the right processes are in place, per-formance must be under control.

In this scenario, reviews are conducted and committees meet with actions tracked. Governance boxes are inevitably ticked. Yet outcomes remain stubbornly unchanged, or in some cases con-tinue to deteriorate despite all of that visible activity.

When this happens, process becomes a substitute for think-ing, meaningful analysis, and corrective action. It creates the appearance of positive "movement" even when underlying issues are left entirely untouched. People become busy managing the system rather than improving it, which is, for anyone who has lived through it, one of the most frustrating and demoralising experiences in organisational life.

This pattern is particularly pronounced in back-end support functions like HR, marketing and technology, where the risk of process without alignment to front-end or customer-driven objectives and priorities is highest.

From the inside, people know with great clarity when a process is helping them think better and when it is simply consuming time and energy without producing anything valuable. When too much effort is spent maintaining process without corresponding improvement in outcomes, cynicism can grow quickly and disengagement often deepens, even among people who genuinely care about the organisation and its purpose. I have often worked in and around organisations where a two-speed culture begins to form; one in which management and frontline realities are so misaligned that the organisation effectively begins to undermine its own chances of sustained success.

How this shows up for individuals

By the time accountability drift has reached this stage, its impact on individuals is unmistakable, even if it is rarely recognised as such. Continually unclear expectations, softened standards, and "nothing to see here" reporting leave people carrying far more uncertainty than necessary.

In this work environment, decisions can often feel heavier for individuals than they should. Judgement and motivation are both eroded because the organisation continues to function day-to-day, and people almost universally assume (incorrectly) that the unspoken problem must lie with them personally. They tell themselves they should be coping better, managing their time more effectively, becoming more resilient. In reality, they are responding entirely rationally and predictably to a system that no longer supports full engagement, clear thinking, or confident decision-making. This is how organisational drift becomes a personal and individual struggle; not through any failure of the individual, but through the accumulated failure of the environment in which the individual is being asked to perform.

Why this stage is so hard to reverse

Once this form of drift is deeply embedded in language, metrics, ineffective processes, and reporting structures, reversing it requires deliberate intervention and a substantial investment of sustained effort. Largely because the signals that once indicated a problem have been normalised. The stories feel familiar, the processes feel entrenched, and the people who question them are at genuine risk of being perceived as negative or disruptive, with the result that most of them have long since stopped raising their hands.

At this point, change requires leaders and boards to do something that feels genuinely counter-intuitive: to *slow down rather than speed up*, to ask more precise and more uncomfortable questions, to be willing to challenge narratives that have become accepted wisdom, and to embed a genuine and organisation-wide commitment to a constructive, honest, and learning-oriented culture reinforced by quality frameworks and accountable leadership.

Why accountability drift persists even when people know something isn't right

By the time drift has embedded itself through language, reporting, and process, most people inside the organisation, including those in governance roles, already sense that something is not quite right.

They may not be able to articulate it clearly, and they may not feel safe naming it publicly, but they undoubtedly feel it on some level.

Decisions feel harder than they should and outcomes can feel less satisfying, even when they are technically acceptable. Conversations feel carefully choreographed rather than genuinely curious. What is striking is that, at this stage, awareness does not automatically lead to action. In fact, I typically see quite the opposite, as fear of the consequences and a clear-eyed awareness of the enormity of the task ahead combine to produce paralysis rather than intervention.

I have seen many situations where capable, thoughtful, and genuinely concerned people choose not to speak up even when they can see the drift clearly. I try to remain hopeful that greater awareness of this dynamic can, over time, begin to change it. However, I have found that this silence is almost never about disengagement. More often, it is a rational calculation: people weigh the cost of raising an issue against the likelihood of it being meaningfully addressed, and factor in the political dynamics, the perceived appetite for challenge, and the personal consequences of being labelled negative or disruptive (as I have been myself).

When past experience, either personal or observed in a peer, suggests that raising concerns leads to whitewashing, explanation, or personal consequences rather than genuine curiosity and change, then silence often becomes an entirely rational response. I have found across my career that very few organisations proactively build a culture that genuinely and consistently encourages people to challenge the status quo, because doing so requires thoughtful processes, well-designed systems, and emotionally intelligent and suitably accountable leadership that consistently model what challenge with respect really looks and feels like. As the old saying goes, common sense is not nearly as common as we tend to assume.

Why this matters for confidence and satisfaction at work

My own professional experience shows clearly that at this stage, the link between organisational drift and personal struggle becomes impossible to ignore. When expectations are unclear, when decision-making feels opaque, and when performance is consistently explained and rationalised rather than honestly examined, people are left carrying far more uncertainty than their roles or responsibilities actually require. I have watched as they expend energy navigating ambiguity and organisational politics that a better-designed system and reliable processes would have rendered unnecessary.

They second-guess themselves in environments that provide insufficient feedback and support, and it's a frustrating and entirely unnecessary waste of energy and resource.

Over time, this can erode confidence in ways that are slow and cumulative and therefore difficult to reverse. People continue to perform, often at a high level, but the work no longer feels as satisfying or meaningful as it once did. The sense of progress is gradually replaced by a sense of endurance, and while the work itself has not changed, the conditions that support good judgement and clear decision-making have quietly and significantly weakened.

Why drift is a leadership issue, not a motivation problem

It is tempting to respond to these dynamics by focusing on *individual* resilience, mindset, or coping strategies. I see leaders whose best interests are often better served by ***not*** challenging the status quo but choose instead to point at individuals who report into them. While those individual-level dynamics certainly have their place, they miss the point entirely.

Struggle at work is rarely the result of insufficient motivation or effort. More often, it is the entirely predictable outcome of systems, leadership weaknesses and organisational frameworks that no longer support clarity, accountability, and learning across the full range of levels from the board downwards.

When organisations allow drift to persist, they place the burden of adaptation on individuals rather than addressing the conditions that create the strain in the first place. That is neither fair nor sustainable, and the chapters ahead are about the practical steps available to any leader who is willing to do something about it.

Drift in accountability and discipline does not take hold because people stop caring. It takes hold because caring people adapt to environments that make clarity progressively harder and challenge progressively more costly, until the adaptation itself becomes so familiar that nobody can quite remember how things were supposed to work.

The purpose of this chapter has been to show how that embedding happens: through reasonable decisions, softened language, familiar processes, and well-intentioned avoidance of discomfort, all accumulating in ways that no single person chose and no single decision produced. Once these patterns are understood and named honestly, they can be interrupted, but only by leaders who are willing to see them clearly and act on what they see.

In the next chapter, we turn to what can practically be done: how to embed the right frameworks and approaches to lift engagement and performance, moving away from diagnosis and toward action. Because while drift is common, it is not inevitable, and every month it continues unchallenged is a month the Discipline Dividend is not compounding.

The organisations that interrupt drift earliest are not simply avoiding a cost. They are reclaiming the compound returns that consistent standards, applied without exception, would have been building all along.

TOOLBOX — Chapter 2: Practical Diagnostic Questions

Identifying the true drivers of performance

A. Questions that identify drift

1. Which performance targets have been revised downward in recent times, and on what basis?
2. Where has "acceptable performance" shifted without an explicit decision or conversation?
3. What problems feel long-standing, when were they first noticed and have they been genuinely and adequately addressed?

B. Questions that test trust bias

1. Which leaders' explanations are rarely if ever challenged, and why?
2. If we are honest, who are the "sacred cows" in our organisation?
3. Where do we rely on confidence and hope as a strategy rather than evidence and scrutiny?
4. How deeply and consistently do we interrogate the drivers of success, not just the causes of failure?

C. Questions that separate narrative from evidence

1. Which assumptions in our organisation are treated as facts without verification?
2. What data would disprove our dominant explanations, and have we looked for it?

3. Where do stories substitute for outcomes, and how have those stories been validated?

D. Questions that expose measurement without control
1. Which KPIs have owners and which have only reporters?
2. Where are explanations accepted without genuine follow-up or consequence?
3. Which dashboards change nothing, and why do they persist?

E. Questions that reveal normalisation
1. What would have alarmed us three years ago that no longer prompts any concern?
2. Which issues are discussed too calmly, or repeatedly glossed over without resolution?
3. What would we refuse to accept if this organisation were brand new?

Closing reflection — Chapter 2

Normalisation of drift is rarely a conscious choice, but identifying it and reversing it must be deliberate, disciplined, and sustained.

Here is a space for your own reflection on this chapter. What resonated with you?

(Write your thoughts here)

____

____

____

____

____

CHAPTER 3

CARRYING THE WEIGHT

"I learned that courage was not the absence of fear, but the triumph over it. The brave man is not he who does not feel afraid, but he who conquers that fear."

—Nelson Mandela,
former President of South Africa

Checked baggage allowance: 23kg.
Leadership baggage: considerably more.

My personal leadership pressure test:

North America, 9/11, and learning to carry the weight

I remember that period of my life all too well. I was in North America, serving as President of the Canadian and US operations for an international Australian listed travel company, in the immediate aftermath of 9/11 – an event that turned our world, and our industry, completely upside-down.

I was turning around a metaphorically sinking ship that had been taking on water for years before I arrived, and I was doing so in the middle of a major realignment and disruption of the entire travel agency business model caused by the 9/11 flow-on effects. At the same time, we were undertaking a major integration and exhaustive business model transformation (both front and back end) across three geographic areas that had previously operated with complete independence from each other and had absolutely no structural alignment between them.

It was our third and final attempt to establish a foothold in the North American market, and we were all learning in real time why the approaches and strategies that had served us so extraordinarily well in Australia and New Zealand simply could not generate the same traction and cut-through in the United States and Canada. This is a very hard lesson that many international businesses discover only after they have already committed themselves fully to those shores.

To add to the complexity, this was my first major international operational leadership role, following my global HR position. And as anyone who knows me well will confirm, I have always been genuinely up for a good transformation challenge. This turnaround was something I passionately believed could be done, and it was absolutely game on from the moment I landed.

Twelve months of immense work and relentless grinding to rebuild just the basic foundations later, and the whole thing felt much more like the Titanic than Apollo Thirteen.

Profitability was only just starting to hint at the green shoots possibility of a potential turnaround, and at a torturously slow pace that satisfied absolutely no one. The pressure from the "mother ship" (otherwise known as our Australian Head Office) was immense, and I could feel it with crushing intensity every minute of every day of every week of the four years I was in that role.

I carried the weight of responsibility for our success, the strategic importance of that market to our broader business and its future, the shareholder and flow-on implications of what was now our third attempt to establish our foothold, and the ongoing responsibility to the people we employed, very heavily on my shoulders. I am not being overly dramatic when I admit that the excruciatingly slow transformation; from the reality of plummeting, rapidly increasing year-on-year losses that I had inherited, through the grinding stabilisation phase, and then finally a painstakingly slow ascent toward consolidated profitability, almost broke me.

For most of that period, I felt incredibly isolated and often profoundly unsupported, without access to the kind of relevant advice and guidance that the situation actually demanded. I often felt like a sitting duck being used for target practice; frequent criticism and regular attacks, but without any constructive input that would actually help me navigate the genuine complexity of the turnaround I was engineering and executing, largely alone.

I worked alongside some exceptional leaders, but at that particular time, none of us knew how to best tackle the specific challenges we were facing in this market. The relevant, contextual, real-time advice I needed, especially at the moments when nothing we tried was working as expected, was simply not available to me. It was profoundly painful to walk that path feeling as isolated and as alone as I often did.

What that experience taught me about control, accountability, and confidence

Looking back now with the benefit of distance and hard-won perspective, that period fundamentally reshaped how I think about leadership, accountability, and what it actually takes to stay confident and decisive when the stakes are genuinely high and the margin for error feels non-existent. At the time, I did not have the language or the framework for what I was experiencing; I simply knew that I was carrying far more than just operational responsibility. I was carrying expectation, pressure, reputational risk, and a very real sense that failure was not an abstract concept but something that would have tangible and lasting consequences for the people I led, for their livelihoods, and for the future of the business.

What became painfully clear to me very early on was how extraordinarily little of the external environment I could genuinely control. I could not control the shockwaves of 9/11 and their ongoing impact on global travel behaviour and the behaviour of our key external stakeholders. I could not control the structural challenges of an industry that was being forced to reinvent itself in real time while everyone was simultaneously fighting for their own survival. I could not control the legacy issues I had inherited, nor the fact that this was our third and final attempt to crack a market that had already resisted us twice before, and which came with its own complex and deeply embedded history. What I *could* control, however, was far less obvious to me at the time and ultimately, far more important.

Learning the difference between responsibility and control

Nobody hands you the controls,
At some point, you just have to fly the thing.

One of the most destabilising realisations of that entire period was the process of recognising the gap between what I was formally responsible for and what I could actually and meaningfully influence. Formally, I was accountable for the performance of the North American business. That accountability was clear, visible, and entirely non-negotiable. Informally, however, I was expected to absorb and manage a range of pressures that sat well outside my direct sphere of control and for a long time, I conflated the two without fully understanding the difference or the cost of doing so.

I felt responsible for outcomes that were being shaped by factors far beyond the realistic reach of any single leader. I internalised criticism that was often rooted in hindsight rather than context. I took on the emotional weight of expectations that were never fully articulated but that I could feel with absolute clarity in every interaction.

That is an extraordinarily exhausting place to operate from for any sustained period of time, and the cumulative mental and physical toll it extracted was significant. Over time, and with those attendant costs making themselves increasingly felt, I began to understand that effective leadership under pressure requires a much sharper and more honest distinction between the two.

Accountability does not mean carrying everything that happens within your remit. It means being brutally and specifically clear about what you can actually influence, what you can genuinely shape, and where your effort will meaningfully move the needle. Without that clarity and focus, responsibility becomes overwhelming rather than empowering and that is *not* a character issue, it is a structural one.

Why the quality of support matters more than we admit

Another profound lesson from that period was how deeply and directly confidence is affected by the quality of support available to you and not just the quantity of experience you bring to the role. By any reasonable measure, I was not inexperienced. I had held senior executive roles before. I understood business, transformation, and complexity in ways that genuinely qualified me for what I had been asked to do. And yet, I found myself repeatedly navigating decisions that had no obvious precedent, with very little relevant guidance to draw on in the moment when I needed it most.

What made that particularly corrosive was not challenge or criticism, because being challenged and stepping up to that challenge is a fundamental part of leadership, and I have never shied away from it. It was criticism without constructive input that did the deeper damage.

Being attacked without being helped is deeply corrosive in a way that is distinct from – and far more damaging than – being pushed hard to perform. When feedback focuses solely on outcomes, without engaging with the complexity of the decisions being made in real time under conditions nobody had encountered before, it does not sharpen judgement. It systematically erodes it.

Over time, you begin to question not just specific decisions, but your own fundamental capability to navigate uncertainty at all. That is not a personal failing. I believe it is a completely predictable outcome of sustained unsupported judgement, and it is far more common in organisational life than leaders are typically willing to acknowledge.

Confidence does not come from certainty

One of the most important insights I carried out of that experience is one I return to constantly: confidence does not come from having all the answers. Certainty is largely an illusion. The conditions are too volatile, the variables too numerous, and the consequences too deeply interdependent for anyone (regardless of their experience or seniority) to feel genuinely sure about much at all.

What sustains confidence in those conditions is something much quieter and much more practical than certainty. It comes from knowing that your decisions are grounded in the best available information at the time they are made. It comes from having tested your assumptions as rigorously as circumstances allow, from having pressure-tested your thinking with people who understand the context and are genuinely prepared to challenge you constructively and offer alternative perspectives, and from being able to say with honest integrity that you have done the work, even when the outcome remains uncertain or does not eventuate in the way you had anticipated.

During that North American turnaround, far too much of that necessary pressure-testing happened inside my own head and let's face it, that's not the best place for it to exist alone. When I felt the situation permitted it and when I did not feel I was unnecessarily exposing my trusted CFO to unnecessary political and emotional noise, we would work through the most complex political issues together. But the structure for thinking that I needed was largely absent, and that absence amplified my doubt in ways I can still feel when I reflect on it. It made my decisions feel much heavier than they needed to.

And at times it transformed professional complexity into something that felt deeply personal; a conflation that serves no leader well and that I have since learned to resist as early and as deliberately as possible.

The hidden cost of carrying decisions alone

Perhaps the most enduring lesson from that period, and one I see repeated with striking regularity in senior leaders today, is the true cost of carrying decisions alone for too long. That cost is not simply fatigue, though fatigue is real and significant. The deeper cost is distortion. When you are operating in sustained isolation, it becomes very easy to lose perspective. You can over-weight certain risks and under-weight others, become more defensive in your thinking – not because you are closed-minded but because you are genuinely tired and worn down – and gradually shift from opening yourself to challenge toward protecting yourself from criticism. None of those shifts improve the quality of decisions. All of them are entirely predictable outcomes of a structure in which the people making the most consequential calls are also the least supported in how they make them.

And yet many organisations still implicitly reward this kind of leadership isolation in subtle ways. Strength is equated not only with self-sufficiency, but an implicit sign of trustworthiness and quiet respect that sometimes garners more implied capability than is perhaps valid.

Conversely, admitting uncertainty is often interpreted as weakness. Asking for help is read as evidence of insufficient capability. My experience taught me precisely the opposite: the strongest and most effective leaders I have encountered and worked with are not the ones who carry everything alone. They are the ones who deliberately build the structures, relationships, and habits that allow them to think clearly under pressure, without the pretence of infallibility that ultimately undermines both their judgement and their credibility.

Why this experience still matters

I share this story because I believe it is increasingly common. I suspect many people reading this have had their own versions; their own war stories and hard-won learnings from periods that tested them in ways they did not fully anticipate and where they were not adequately supported to navigate. What likely unites most of those experiences is that the scale and complexity of decisions people are expected to make at work has grown significantly over the past decade, while the quality of real-time support available to them has not kept pace.

This gap has been further amplified by the emergence and disruption of AI and the cascading changes it is producing in every aspect of how organisations operate. As a result, many capable professionals find themselves carrying responsibility without reinforcement, accountability without clarity, and pressure without perspective. I believe that combination is, without exception, a breeding ground for unnecessary struggle.

What I learned in North America, painfully and excruciatingly slowly, is that leadership confidence is not a personality trait and it is not something that can be summoned through sheer force of character. It is an outcome of clearly defined systems, of adequate and contextually relevant support, and of disciplined thinking habits built deliberately rather than assumed to exist. When those conditions are present, even the most complex challenges feel navigable. When they are absent, even the most experienced and genuinely capable leaders begin to doubt themselves in ways that compound into something much more serious than a temporary dip in confidence.

Why organisations confuse accountability with control

What took me considerably longer to fully understand, is how frequently accountability and control are conflated in practice, regardless of how clearly people claim to understand the distinction.

In theory, most senior leaders would agree that accountability and control are different things. In practice, the two are blurred almost immediately once real pressure and genuine complexity enter the system. Accountability is assigned formally through organisational structures where titles are granted, roles are defined, expectations are set.

From that point on, however, responsibility tends to expand quietly, absorbing not just what the person can meaningfully influence, but everything that falls within their nominal remit, whether or not they have the authority, the information, or the adequate support to affect those outcomes in any meaningful way. Over time, that expansion becomes normal and unremarked upon. People stop asking whether someone actually controls an outcome and focus instead on whether they are formally accountable for it as though the two are the same thing. They are not, and the distinction matters.

What is compounding this problem is the constantly evolving nature of structure itself, and the inadequate attention paid to the flow-on implications every structural change has on existing role definitions and responsibilities.

How often do organisations genuinely and thoroughly reset role responsibilities, KPIs, and decision rights when a new structure is introduced or a reporting line changes?

The research on role clarity and team performance is unequivocal on this point:

> *Teams with clear, stable goals and well-understood responsibilities and reliable processes consistently outperform those operating in ambiguity, and when performance measures are precise, sensitive to what people can actually control, and paired with explicit role clarity, people experience the system as fairer and are significantly more motivated to deliver against it.*

Across thirty years of experience, I have seen this done properly and consistently exactly once.

In the vast majority of organisations I have worked with and inside, structures and roles shift continuously, with minimal attention paid to maintaining optimal alignment throughout the business as they do. Accountability blurs, responsibilities overlap, and what should be clean lines of ownership quickly become a tangled web that nobody chose and everyone navigates in their own way.

ur org chart is so complex that nobody can actually find the organisation in it.

How this shows up in day-to-day leadership

I see this most clearly, and most damagingly, in how performance conversations unfold at every level of the organisation. A leader is held to account for results that are being materially shaped by multiple interconnected systems, legacy decisions, market dynamics, and behaviours that sit well beyond their direct reach. At the same time, they may have limited practical influence over resourcing, capability development, structural constraints, or the realistic pace at which meaningful change is possible in their environment. When outcomes disappoint as they inevitably do in any organisation operating in complex conditions, the response is rarely to interrogate the system that produced the sub-optimal outcome with genuine curiosity. Instead, attention turns to the individual: what they should have done differently, what they failed to anticipate, how they might need to "step up" or be moved on.

This framing feels decisive, and it is often presented as evidence of a healthy performance culture. In reality, it is frequently misleading and consistently misses the nuance of the true underlying cause of the performance gap.

It places the weight of systemic complexity squarely on individual shoulders, while leaving the underlying structural drivers and organisational responsibilities entirely untouched, which means that the next person placed into the same conditions will face exactly the same dynamic, and probably produce a similar outcome.

Why this undermines good judgement

When people are held accountable for things they cannot genuinely control, something subtle but profoundly important happens to their decision-making over time. They become risk-averse in some areas and overly defensive in others. They begin optimising for perception and self-preservation rather than for substance and quality outcomes. They focus increasing energy on protecting themselves from criticism rather than opening themselves to the kind of challenge that would actually improve their thinking.

This is not a reflection of insufficient courage or integrity on their part. It is the entirely rational and predictable response of a capable person operating in an environment where the cost of being wrong feels disproportionate and where honest uncertainty is not rewarded. I have found that people default, in those conditions, to what feels safest politically and environmentally rather than what is most operationally effective. They choose options that are easiest to justify and that make their work life less exposed, rather than those most likely to genuinely address root causes.

This is one of the quietest and most consistent ways organisations slowly lose their edge; not through dramatic failure, but through the accumulation of risk-minimising, politically calibrated decisions made by people who would, in a healthier environment, have made very different choices.

How confused accountability feeds drift

This confusion between accountability and control feeds directly into the drift described in detail in the previous chapter, and it does so in a self-reinforcing cycle that is extremely difficult to interrupt once it has been running for any length of time. When leaders are expected to own outcomes without being given adequate means to influence them, explanations and context inevitably proliferate to fill the gap. The narratives that we start to use tend to soften and create a protective shield. As individuals, we simultaneously internalise pressure that should properly be addressed systemically, often assuming that if we were simply better, smarter, or more resilient, things would feel less impossible than they do.

That assumption is, in the vast majority of cases I have encountered, not true and it is certainly not helpful. We all perform as well as our work environments and their supporting ecosystems enable and support us to perform. The issue is not personal capacity. It is structural misalignment between what people are asked to own and what they are genuinely supported to influence.

Why this is so hard to address openly

Part of the reason this dynamic persists is that questioning it can feel genuinely threatening to everyone involved. To ask honestly whether someone truly controls an outcome they have been held accountable for is to question role design, governance structures, decision rights, and power distribution simultaneously and those are challenging, uncomfortable conversations in any organisation, but especially in organisations that pride themselves on clarity and accountability and whose leaders have strong personal identities built around those values.

> *It can feel far easier and considerably less risky to maintain the comfortable fiction that accountability equals control than to acknowledge the gaps between formal responsibility, practical authority, and realistic influence.*

But those gaps are precisely where unnecessary disconnect and struggle quietly take root and where the Discipline Dividend is being quietly and consistently destroyed.

What I learned to do differently

The North America experience forced me to confront this distinction in an extraordinarily personal way, and to sit with the discomfort of it for long enough that it genuinely changed how I operated from that point forward. I had to learn, sometimes the very hard way, to clearly separate what I could meaningfully influence from what I could not, and to focus my energy as deliberately and as relentlessly as possible on the former. That discipline did not remove my accountability for the overall outcomes; it changed how I carried it, and that change was significant in practice.

It allowed me to make decisions with greater integrity and less second-guessing, even when outcomes were slow to improve. It helped me resist the temptation to absorb criticism that was not grounded in the actual reality of what I was navigating. And it reminded me in ways I have never forgotten, that leadership is not about performing control over everything that falls within your remit, but about acting decisively and with full commitment in the areas where genuine influence exists and where focused effort will actually move the needle.

Importantly, it also gave me a much clearer and more useful framework for helping my own teams focus their energy in a similar way, by concentrating on what they could most directly affect while building more effective systems to mitigate the factors that were genuinely outside anyone's control.

That distinction became foundational to everything that followed.

Why this matters beyond extreme situations

It would be easy to read the North America story and conclude that its lessons are specific to extreme circumstances, be they major crises, catastrophic market disruptions, or large-scale turnarounds of the kind that most leaders will never be asked to manage.

That conclusion would be a mistake, and I want to be clear about why. I see these same dynamics playing out, more quietly but no less significantly, in everyday organisational life.

I see them in projects that stall for no immediately obvious reason, in teams that quietly underperform despite being filled with capable people, in roles that feel disproportionately heavy relative to their apparent complexity, and in leaders who are visibly at the point of exhaustion without being able to explain to themselves or anyone else how they arrived there.

Whenever I have seen accountability assigned without corresponding clarity about control and without the structures and support needed to enable genuine influence over the outcomes in question, confidence has eroded and struggle has increased. The scale and the specific circumstances may differ enormously, but the underlying dynamic is always the same.

How control, accountability, and confidence are actually rebuilt

The most important realisation that emerged from my North America experience, and one that has shaped every engagement and every role I have taken on since, is that confidence at work is not something you can simply summon through personality, resilience, or sheer force of professional will. Yes, these qualities serve you well in complex and genuinely stressful situations, and I would never dismiss their importance.

But confidence is fundamentally built or eroded by the conditions in which decisions are made, and those conditions are designable by the leaders. When people are clear about what they genuinely control, adequately supported in how they think through high-stakes decisions, and held accountable in ways that are fair, honest, and grounded in operational reality, confidence tends to grow naturally and organically, compounding over time in the same way that any well-supported capability does.

That, in its most personally felt form, is the Discipline Dividend; not a corporate framework but a real and practical experience of what clarity, real support, and fair accountability produce in the confidence and sustained capability of the people operating within those conditions. When those conditions are absent, even the most objectively capable and experienced professionals begin to second-guess themselves and fail to reach their full potential.

It is almost always because the system around them lacks what they need.

Let me state it plainly one more time, because I believe it matters: this is not, in most cases, a character issue. When a capable person is struggling with confidence in their decision-making, it is rarely because they lack what it takes.

Why experience alone is not enough

As we have discussed, there is a persistent and understandable assumption in organisations that experience should automatically translate into confidence; namely that the more you have seen, the more patterns you have encountered, and the deeper your track record, the more easily you should be able to navigate complexity without needing significant support.

In many recruitment processes, we actively select for this expectation, sometimes at the expense of other qualities that matter just as much. The assumption has surface logic, but it does not hold under examination. Experience without the right reinforcement and thinking support can actually make things considerably harder rather than easier.

Experienced leaders often carry a deeper and more finely calibrated awareness of risk than their less experienced counterparts. They understand the potential consequences of decisions more fully. They can see second and third-order effects that others miss entirely.

But without adequate thinking support from the environment around them, that enhanced awareness does not reliably produce greater confidence. In reality I have seen it frequently produce greater hesitation, more internal conflict, and a paradoxical increase in the sense that the stakes are too high and the margin for error too thin.

I have seen this pattern play out repeatedly, both in myself at various points in my career and in many of the leaders I have worked closely with. The issue is almost never lack of capability. It is the absence of the structural support that would allow that capability to be used to its full and intended potential.

How better support changes the quality of judgement

What would have made the greatest practical difference to me during that North American turnaround was not more authority or reduced accountability. It was better support for thinking – not generic advice, not hindsight critique offered without any constructive alternative to consider, but relevant, contextually aware challenge and genuine reinforcement at the moment decisions were being shaped and constructed.

When leaders have access to that kind of support, the quality of judgement improves in ways that are both visible and measurable. Decisions become cleaner and more clearly grounded. Trade-offs are understood and explicitly weighed rather than avoided. The thinking that underpins choices can be articulated with clarity and genuine confidence, rather than defended with the brittle certainty of someone who knows they are largely guessing. Importantly, better thinking support does not remove pressure; the pressure of complex decisions in high-stakes environments is simply part of the work, and any leader who tells you otherwise is either not facing decisions of real consequence or not being honest with you.

However, what it does is make pressure far more manageable, because the weight is genuinely shared and the thinking is genuinely tested before it is committed to.

In my experience this practical support for better decision making is always highly evident in high-performing teams, where face-to-face collaboration forms the basis of day-to-day rhythms and well designed communication processes. This can be as simple as allocating a small amount of time in daily stand-ups to raising issues and asking for ideas to solve them in this group setting. From a leadership perspective, this creates the expectation and permission for others to follow this approach throughout their work days.

At the risk of being controversial, I believe it is almost impossible to do this to the same level of genuine personal connection and emotional investment via slack and other online channels.

Why carrying decisions alone Is still so common

Despite everything we understand and can articulate about decision quality and the conditions that support it, many organisations continue to operate as though isolation is a natural and appropriate feature of seniority. As roles become more senior and more consequential, the formal and informal support available to the people in them tends to diminish rather than increase. Expectations rise, complexity deepens, but the structures that support good thinking, which I have found to be genuine peer challenge, contextually relevant mentoring, space for honest uncertainty, all quietly disappear, replaced by the implicit cultural expectation that senior leaders should "have it covered" and should not need to ask for help.

This creates a genuinely strange paradox at the very top of most organisations: the people making the most consequential decisions, with the widest reach and the most significant downstream consequences, are in many cases the least structurally supported in how they make those decisions. And they often feel the greatest personal and professional pressure to appear confident and certain even when they are operating with inadequate information, insufficient challenge, and no real time to properly think before they are required to act.

Over time, that paradox produces exactly the behaviours organisations claim they want to eliminate, specifically defensive decision-making, over-reliance on precedent and past patterns, growing aversion to challenge, and a quiet but deepening reluctance to admit uncertainty or genuinely engage with alternative approaches. None of it improves outcomes. All of it is a predictable response to a structure that was never designed to support the kind of thinking that the most important decisions actually require.

How this links back to discipline

When people describe being disconnected and struggling at work, they most commonly frame it in terms of being overwhelmed, burnt out, or simply stretched beyond what feels sustainable. Those experiences are entirely real, and I do not want to minimise how serious they are for the people living through them.

But underneath those experiences is almost always something more specific, and more addressable, than the broad labels suggest. People are struggling because they are carrying responsibility without reinforcement, accountability without clarity, and pressure without any disciplined way of separating what they can genuinely control from what they cannot.

In other words, they are being asked to deliver outcomes inside systems that lack discipline: discipline in defining roles, in setting expectations, in how decisions are supported, and in how performance is judged. When that discipline is absent, work becomes a daily endurance exercise rather than a meaningful engagement with work that matters, and accountability turns from a source of agency into a burden that many capable people quite rationally decide to put down.

When discipline is present and consistently practised, the opposite happens: responsibility is still real, but it is reinforced; accountability is still serious, but it is fair and bounded; confidence is still hard-won, but it is supported rather than eroded.

That difference is the beginning of the Discipline Dividend in action.

Closing Chapter 3

What I learned in North America, painfully and over the course of four of the most formative years of my professional life, is that leadership confidence is not about knowing everything or exercising control over the uncontrollable. It is about the disciplined work of knowing where to focus, being genuinely supported in how you think, and consistently being held accountable in ways that are fair, transparent, and grounded in what you can actually influence.

When those conditions are present, even the most genuinely complex challenges feel navigable; definitely not easy, but navigable and when they are absent, struggle becomes not just likely but inevitable, regardless of the capability and commitment of the individual being asked to carry it.

In this book, I call the upside of those conditions the Discipline Dividend: the compound return you get when clarity, support and fair accountability are designed in on purpose rather than left to chance.

It *always* shows up in better decisions, more honest conversations, and leaders who can sustain confidence without burning themselves or their teams out.

In the chapters that follow, we move away from diagnosis and towards clear, practical actions which are the specific disciplines any leader can bring into their own organisation to begin rebuilding the conditions that support confidence, clarity, and genuine accountability. We will look at what is realistically within our control, how better thinking support changes outcomes in practice, and how tools including AI can be used to strengthen judgement rather than replace it. What this book is ultimately about is not simply identifying the problem, but building the disciplined architecture that allows the Discipline Dividend to show up, reliably, in everyday work.

TOOLBOX — Chapter 3

Questions to examine control, accountability, confidence, and decision load

These questions are designed to help you surface where responsibility, control, and confidence may be misaligned; for yourself, your role, or your organisation as a whole. They are best answered slowly, honestly, and revisited over time as circumstances evolve.

A. Questions to clarify what you truly control

1. Which outcomes am I formally accountable for that are being materially shaped by factors outside my direct control?

2. Where am I expending significant emotional or cognitive energy on issues I cannot realistically influence?

3. What aspects of my role genuinely allow me to shape outcomes, and where is my influence more indirect than I typically assume?

4. If I were forced to name only the three areas where my focused effort most directly affects results, what would they be?

5. Where might I be conflating responsibility with control, and what is the real cost of doing that?

B. Questions to surface unsupported accountability

1. Where am I being held accountable for outcomes without access to the information, authority, or support needed to influence them properly?

2. What feedback do I receive that focuses on outcomes without genuinely engaging with the complexity of the decisions made in real time?
3. Where do I feel criticised or attacked rather than constructively challenged?
4. Which decisions feel the heaviest, and what does that say about the quality of support around them?
5. Who, if anyone, do I genuinely pressure-test my thinking with before decisions are locked in?

C. Questions to examine confidence at work
1. When I reflect honestly on my confidence at work, does it come from genuine certainty, or from knowing I have thought things through as rigorously as conditions allow?
2. In which situations do I feel most grounded and confident, and what conditions are consistently present in those moments?
3. Where do I notice self-doubt appearing, even when I am objectively capable of the work being asked of me?
4. How often do I replay decisions privately after the fact, and what is the cost of carrying that habit?
5. What would need to change in my environment for confidence to feel more genuinely grounded and less performative?

D. Questions about carrying decisions alone
1. Which decisions am I currently carrying largely in isolation?
2. What prevents me from involving others earlier in my thinking; is it time pressure, political dynamics, fear of judgement, or established habit?
3. Where have I equated self-sufficiency with strength, even when it may be quietly undermining the quality of my decisions?

4. If I were better supported in how I think, which decisions
    would feel genuinely lighter?
5. What is the long-term cost of continuing to carry this level
    of decision load alone?

**E. Questions to test organisational alignment between account-
ability and control**
1. Where in this organisation are people routinely held
    accountable without corresponding clarity about control or
    genuine influence?
2. How often are role responsibilities, KPIs, and decision rights
    revisited when structures or reporting lines change?
3. Where do organisational narratives explain outcomes rather
    than honestly interrogate causes?
4. What issues recur despite repeated effort, and what does that
    suggest about structural misalignment?
5. For accountability and control to be properly aligned in this
    organisation, what would genuinely need to change?

F. Questions that reframe confidence as a system outcome
1. Do we treat confidence as a personal trait, or as something
    actively shaped by systems, support, and role clarity?
2. How well does this organisation support good thinking
    before decisions are made, rather than critiquing them after
    outcomes are known?
3. Where would better pressure-testing of key decisions
    improve outcomes without slowing necessary momentum?
4. What forms of support actually strengthen confidence and
    capability here and which merely create noise and activ-
    ity?
5. How could we measurably reduce unnecessary struggle by
    improving how high-stakes decisions are supported?

Closing Reflection — Chapter 3

Confidence is not about knowing everything. It is about knowing where to focus, being genuinely supported in how you think, and being held accountable for what you can realistically and meaningfully influence. Struggle at work most often begins when those conditions are absent and not because people are weak or lacking, but because the systems around them are misaligned in ways that make their best work unnecessarily hard.

Here is a space for your own reflection on this chapter. What resonated with you?

(Write your thoughts here)
____

____

____

____

____

CHAPTER 4

WHY GOOD LEADERS STOPPED HOLDING THE LINE

"If you just set out to be liked, you would be prepared to compromise on anything at any time. And you would achieve nothing."

— Margaret Thatcher,
former Prime Minister of the United Kingdom

When I arrived in New York to begin the work of rebuilding the North American business, one of the first and most important decisions I had to make was who would be around me when I did it.

We were integrating three geographically separate divisions across Canada and the United States that had previously operated with full autonomy, each running their own back-end functions, their own culture, their own way of doing things. The task was to consolidate all of that into a single, centralised North American structure capable of executing one of the most complex transformations I had ever been asked to lead. We were, quite literally, starting with a blank whiteboard.

Time was not on our side. The consolidated business was losing increasingly significant amounts of money across all three regions, and every week that passed without a functioning unified structure was a week the losses deepened. I needed to move quickly on the team, and I needed to get it right.

I have always operated on the same philosophy when building executive teams: hire the smartest possible people with the strongest values and cultural alignment, and deliberately select those who are capable of challenging your thinking openly and consistently. I have no time for people who leave things unsaid, who smooth over problems to keep the peace, or who tell you what you want to hear rather than what you need to know. In a turnaround of the scale we were attempting, I needed people who were genuinely better than me in their respective domains and who were honest enough to say so when it mattered.

I was extremely fortunate at that point in time. There was an abundance of talented, energetic, and genuinely capable leaders to choose from, some drawn from our existing North American operations, others from our Australian head office. The team that came together was, and I say this without any qualification, the finest executive team I have ever had the privilege of working with. Deeply capable. Culturally aligned. Fiercely committed to the mission.

When we gathered for our very first business planning workshop in New York; a brand new team, many of us with zero direct experience in this market, no reliable consolidated reporting to work from, and almost no answers to the questions we needed to answer, it was, by any objective measure, an absolute bin fire.

But what we lacked in information, process, and certainty, we more than made up for in the quality of the people in that room. I knew, within the first hour of that first meeting, that we had something genuinely special to work with.

What I did not anticipate was the series of events that would test us all in ways I had not prepared for.

Bringing key executives from Australia to work in North America carries with it a particular set of vulnerabilities that anyone who has led an internationally dispersed team will recognise immediately. Life happens. Families back home experience health crises. Partners who committed to the adventure discover, sometimes within weeks or months, that they are not willing to sustain it. One of my most critical functional executive roles turned over not once during the four years, but several times. Each departure entirely understandable, each one leaving me to make another appointment under pressure and at pace.

The final replacement started promisingly. They settled into the role, connected with the team, and the early signals were positive. Then, quickly, small cracks appeared. There were some health issues that had not been evident at appointment. And I started hearing feedback – a mix of genuinely positive assessments from some of their team members, and notably negative feedback from others.

Here is where I made my mistake. And I want to be clear-eyed about this, because the entire argument of this chapter rests on my being honest about it.

I looked at that mix of equally positive and negative feedback and I rationalised it into neutrality. I told myself it balanced out and that mixed feedback was not unusual in a complex, high-pressure environment. I told myself I would watch the situation more closely but that I did not yet have enough to act on. Essentially, I chose the easier option.

For approximately six months, I did not pursue the direct, disciplined conversations with that leader and their team that would have identified the real dynamic far sooner. By the time I finally paused long enough to genuinely investigate, the damage had been done in ways that were significantly harder to address than they would have been at month two.

What I eventually identified and what I now recognise immediately when I encounter it, was classically narcissistic leadership behaviour. A pattern in which an individual actively cultivates relationships with those they identify as able to advance their career or reflect positively on their performance, while systematically ignoring and disrespecting those they perceive as unable to serve that purpose. The result is an unusually extreme spread of feedback: exceptional ratings from some, damning ones from others, with almost nothing in the middle. It shows up on 360-degree surveys as something that looks, on the surface, like a polarising style until you trace exactly who is having which experience, and why.

I did not recognise what I was seeing in time. The individual eventually left the role, but the learning I took from that period has stayed with me in every leadership situation since.

The most important thing I did wrong was not the initial misread, but the rationalisation. The moment I looked at the conflicting feedback and chose the interpretation that required less of me and made it easier to move on to the next problem on the list. I had stopped doing my job to protect my people from poor leadership. It wasn't dramatic or obvious. Just quiet abdication with entirely understandable intent, in a way that compounded over months into something that was entirely avoidable.

That is exactly how I have learned that discipline breaks down, even for good leaders. Through the same pattern of accumulated small decisions, I described in Chapter 2. Each are defensible in isolation, costly in aggregate and clearly, in hindsight, preventable.

Research on leadership derailment tracking more than 300 senior leaders *across a multi-decade programme of research at the Center for Creative Leadership*, found that the most common cause of executive failure was not lack of intelligence or poor strategy. It was the inability to build and maintain effective relationships with key stakeholders, combined with a failure to act on clear performance information in time to change outcomes. The leaders in those studies were not negligent. They were, almost without exception, trying to be fair. What they were not doing was holding the line with the consistency that fairness actually requires.

The pattern I have seen in every organisation since

What that North American experience gave me was a lens I have never been able to set aside. I now see variations of the same dynamic; the rationalisation, the delayed intervention, the compounding cost in virtually every organisation I work with, regardless of size, sector, or level of sophistication.

The specific circumstances change, however the underlying pattern typically does not.

Consider this scenario:

A highly relational COO oversees a business unit led by a long-serving executive who is widely liked and known to be under significant personal strain. Results have been drifting for several quarters, but the narrative explanations are persuasive; market volatility, a key client loss, a difficult integration. The COO recognises the drift. She also recognises that the timing feels wrong, that the relationship feels too important to risk, that a direct conversation feels harsh given the circumstances. She defers taking action and then defers again. By the time a formal intervention happens, the high performers in that business unit have already quietly disengaged, having spent months watching standards slide without consequence. The adjacent teams have normalised their workarounds and the "water-cooler" conversations that highlight the issue have been flowing abundantly.

At this point, the culture has accommodated the under-performance into its operating rhythm.

And the executive himself, when finally confronted, is genuinely blindsided because no-one had ever clearly and directly told him, in a way that felt real, that his position was in genuine jeopardy.

That is a composite story drawn from multiple organisations I have worked with closely. But the COO in it is not a weak leader. She is not indifferent, negligent, or lacking in courage. She is trying to be kind and fair while weighing a complex set of legitimate considerations and making the decision that causes the least immediate harm.

The problem is that the least *immediate* harm and the least *total* harm are not the same thing. And the gap between them is where avoidance lives.

Why the other extreme is not the answer

Before we go further, I want to be direct about something. The argument I am making in this chapter is not an argument for hard-edged, punitive, metric-driven performance management. I have seen and personally lived through that version of discipline, and it is equally damaging, just in a different direction.

The Wells Fargo cross-selling scandal is perhaps the most instructive example of what discipline without ethics, psychological safety, or basic human dignity produces. For years, frontline staff were pushed to meet aggressive product quotas: eight products per household, under relentless monitoring and the ever-present threat of disciplinary action or termination for missing targets. From the outside, this looked like rigorous accountability: clear metrics, real consequences, no ambiguity about expectations.

In reality, it was coercive pressure in which there was no space to raise concerns, no mechanism for challenge, and no pathway to express the reality that the targets were unachievable without crossing ethical lines. Employees opened millions of unauthorised accounts simply to survive in what one described as a pressure cooker culture. The bank eventually paid billions in fines and settlements. The reputational damage was incalculable.

When I place that story alongside the COO composite example above, the lesson becomes clear: both extremes are forms of failed leadership, even though they look entirely different on the surface. One avoids necessary conversations in the name of compassion. The other weaponises accountability in the name of performance. Neither produces the culture of genuine, sustained high performance that I am advocating for, and both carry significant legal and organisational consequences.

The ideal discipline I am describing sits between those two failure modes. It is timely rather than delayed and specific rather than punitive. It is explicit rather than implied and is delivered consistently as a normal, ongoing feature of how people are led, rather than as a rare, high-stakes event reserved for crisis moments.

How empathy quietly becomes avoidance – mind the gap

When discipline breaks down in an organisation, it is consistently the case that the leaders responsible are typically good people trying to do the right thing with genuine empathy. The individual circumstances they were weighing were often legitimately complex.

So the problem is not the empathy; it is the indefinite extension of it and the transformation of what should have been a temporary adjustment in pace and support into a permanent suspension of the expectation itself. Time easily stretches out from days to months to years, further embedding the issue.

I have found that it tends to follow a recognisable sequence; expectations are initially clear but then something subtly shifts or changes. This can include context, performance, health, or personal circumstances. Then I see the leader usually responds by holding off on difficult conversations (as I have done personally and will dive into in the next chapter), or by quietly adjusting expectations without any explicit discussion about what has changed and what has not.

Over the following six to twelve months, you can observe other people in the system notice the gap between what is said and what is tolerated, and they adjust their own standards accordingly. What began as kindness becomes, in practice, a form of organisational neglect. I frequently observe a quiet redistribution of workloads; often with high performers carrying more weight and with diminishing enthusiasm. At this point, organisational trust in whether standards are applied fairly begins to erode fairly rapidly. The original individual is not set up to succeed; they are simply protected from honest feedback until the problem becomes impossible to ignore. At which point, any intervention feels abrupt, disproportionate, and punitive rather than developmental.

When you hear people expressing genuine surprise at negative performance feedback when they are being managed out of a role, that is almost always a reliable signal that this sequence has played out somewhere in the organisation's recent history.

I know, because I have been both the leader who let that sequence develop and the one who was brought in to address its consequences. Neither position is comfortable.

What the research confirms and where it gets misread

The academic framing that has perhaps most significantly contributed to leaders' confusion about discipline is the concept of psychological safety. Amy Edmondson's foundational work on high-performing teams is excellent and important. But it has been widely and consistently misread and mis-applied in ways that have actively undermined organisational discipline.

Psychological safety is not the absence of pressure, challenge, or accountability. It is, in Edmondson's original terms, the belief that people will not be punished or humiliated for speaking up with ideas, questions, concerns, or mistakes.

Edmondson's research is crystal clear on one point that is often conveniently ignored in popular summaries: high psychological safety on its own does not produce high performance. The teams that performed best in her studies sat in what she calls the learning zone, specifically where **high psychological safety and high accountability exist together**.

What many organisations have done instead is to lower standards in the name of "safety", creating exactly the apathy zone her work warns about: low accountability, low challenge, lots of language about care, and very little disciplined follow-through.

The highest-performing teams Edmondson studied were not teams where standards were soft or expectations were flexible. They were teams where standards were high *and* people felt safe to name problems, question assumptions, and admit uncertainty without fear of being punished for honesty. I have seen this play out in my own experience being part of, and working with high-performing teams around the globe.

What many organisations have done with that research is to conflate psychological safety with emotional comfort, and to use the former as a justification for avoiding the latter. The result is organisations in which standards are softened to avoid conflict, where expectations are left implicit to avoid discomfort, and where the absence of discipline is reframed as a cultural strength.

Let me re-state: it is not. It is a cultural vulnerability, and it is becoming *more* exposed, not less, as the operating environment becomes more transparent.

Professor Arthur Brooks, among others, has argued consistently that people derive genuine meaning from competence, agency, and progress, not from comfort. When organisations remove the disciplined expectation of performance in the name of wellbeing, they often remove the very conditions under which wellbeing flourishes. People need to know what is expected of them. They need to see effort recognised and under-performance addressed in a consistent manner across the organisation and to believe that the system is fair.

None of those needs are met by a culture that prioritises the avoidance of difficult conversations and effective accountability.

What disciplined environments actually look like

When I walk into an organisation that has built a genuinely disciplined culture, specifically one that combines high expectations with genuine care for the people expected to meet them, a number of things become immediately visible.

Ownership is almost always explicit and unambiguous. In disciplined environments, there is never any real uncertainty about who is accountable for a specific outcome, however shared input is valued and encouraged. Shared accountability without a single clear owner is recognised as a mechanism for diffusing responsibility until it belongs to no-one.

A previous founder/CEO I worked with was excellent at flushing out where these accountability gaps existed and taught me many lessons. When sitting in a meeting room with groups of executives dissecting poor results, he would relentlessly keep asking the same question over and over until we determined an answer: "who is ultimately responsible for this result?"

Not a team, not a working group but a *single senior executive* was the only acceptable answer and the relentless and often uncomfortable way he probed into this until he identified the true owner (or obvious lack thereof) was a learning insight into true and clear accountability.

Hard conversations in disciplined cultures are frequent and often brief, because they happen close to the work rather than accumulating into a delayed and emotionally loaded confrontation. The absence of drama is not a sign that nothing is being addressed; usually it is a sign that things are being addressed before they become dramatic.

In disciplined work environments, I also observe that metrics serve clear decisions rather than driving generic narratives. When a small number of meaningful indicators are tracked, discussed honestly, and used as prompts for curiosity and early action rather than evidence for explanations that have already been constructed, real magic and business growth is enabled. When a metric moves, the first question is rightly "what might be driving this?", not "whose fault is this?". When the focus shifts to WHY metrics are moving (both positively and negatively) through a sense of genuine curiosity, while still combined with clear accountability, everyone benefits and learns from the discussion and interaction. It's a clear win-win scenario.

Let me reiterate that it is as important to take the time to interrogate the drivers of great results as it is to dig into poor results. Far too often we gloss over trying to better understand the underlying drivers of great results and whether they were the outcome of factors within or outside our control. This critical deeper knowledge helps us to understand how to deliver better, more consistent results moving forward. Without this reflection and analysis, results become inconsistent and we discover over time (to our detriment) that those we assumed were deliberately being driven by internal actions were, in fact, caused by factors outside our control. The rot of overconfidence and false positive narratives accompanying results quickly sets in.

In complex, changing environments, expectations also require regular re-articulation, particularly when structures change, roles evolve, or the strategic context shifts. I have seen organisations execute major restructures without meaningfully updating the role expectations, KPIs, or decision rights of a single affected position and those who report in and around them. In all honesty, I have done it myself.

In these cases, the organisational chart changes (often quite dramatically) but the operating model does not, resulting in a widening gap where clarity and accountability quietly disappear. This is far more common and impactful that we often understand for some valid reasons.

Pre- the AI-era, the time and manual resources required to ensure full organisational alignment through updated impacted PDs and KPIs every time a major or minor restructure occurs were significant and thus often avoided. Thankfully, accessible AI tools now mean this can be done quickly and efficiently and the challenge is to add this expectation to the roles and responsibilities of HR professionals.

The hidden costs that nobody adds up

The real cost of doing nothing has never once appeared in a budget. Until now.

When discipline breaks down, the organisation stops earning its Discipline Dividend.

As we have all witnessed, the cost of this break down rarely shows up immediately or obviously in the financial statements. It first appears in how people experience their work, in culture then in behaviour, and eventually compounds (often much later) in the numbers.

At an individual level, I consistently observe a significant increase in cognitive and mental load as people attempt to second-guess expectations that were never explicitly stated. This can result in rises in anxiety often mislabelled as burnout, because genuine ambiguity about standards is genuinely extremely exhausting to navigate on a day-to-day basis. Even high performers and those most passionately engaged in the business begin to disengage quietly. They remain productive, but the discretionary effort and enthusiasm that produce exceptional rather than adequate outcomes gradually diminish.

At an organisational level, decision-making slows and issues are repeatedly discussed but never fully resolved. Convenient and untested narratives can easily become embedded without adequate or appropriate scrutiny. The organisational "noise" proliferates through more reporting, more process, more meetings and generally more continual "fire-fighting" activity as a substitute for the early, clear intervention that would have made most of the noise unnecessary.

Regardless of the drivers, when performance becomes person-dependent rather than system-reliable, we have created a condition in which its results are essentially hostage to the motivation and behaviour of specific individuals, rather than embedded in a structure that produces consistent standards.

This then is the accumulated cost of the many rationalisations along the way, where it is impossible to identify any single conversation that was avoided, but where the compound interest of them all is glaringly obvious.

What AI is about to make more visible

I want to close this chapter with a thought that will be developed further later in this book, but that belongs here because it changes the stakes of the argument I have been making.

The progressive integration of AI-enabled analytics into organisational governance and leadership practices is about to make the patterns described in this chapter significantly harder to sustain undetected. Metric drift and trend analysis, the gradual migration of reported indicators away from the ones that would most clearly signal a problem, is precisely the kind of pattern that AI is now capable of identifying across reporting periods, long before it reaches the severity that would trigger a human intervention. When pointed in the right direction, early signals of disengagement, team dysfunction, and performance drift are increasingly visible in the data that organisations already are starting to collect, if anyone is looking at it with the right tools and the right questions.

This is, depending on your perspective, either an opportunity or a threat. For leaders who have been operating with a deliberate intent to deliver optimal levels of discipline and transparency, it is a significant competitive advantage and gives them the ability to detect and address drift earlier, more specifically, and with less reliance on informal observation and political judgement. For leaders who have been managing through a narrative-driven approach, deferring difficult conversations and quietly cultivating comfortable ambiguity in their organisations, AI is bringing forward a reckoning that is arriving regardless of readiness.

My firm belief is that AI does not remove the need for disciplined leadership. Instead, it is effectively removing the places where the absence of it can hide.

The conversation that needed to happen six months ago is not made easier by better data. It is made more urgent. The discipline to have it remains, as it has always been, entirely human. And it is that discipline: daily, consistent, architectural, and non-negotiable that generates the returns this book is about.

The Discipline Dividend is not earned in a single courageous conversation. It is earned in the thousand small ones that precede it, making the organisation the kind of place where the courageous conversation, when it finally arrives, already feels like the norm.

TOOLBOX — Chapter 4

Questions to diagnose discipline, accountability, and avoidance in practice

Use these to surface where discipline may have softened, been avoided, or been misapplied in yourself, your team, or your organisation. Answer them slowly and honestly.

A. Where discipline has quietly broken down
1. Where have expectations been allowed to remain implicit rather than clearly stated?
2. Which performance issues are repeatedly contextualised but never directly addressed?
3. What conversations have been deferred "for now" that have remained unresolved for months?
4. Where have standards shifted without being explicitly discussed or agreed?
5. What behaviours are currently being tolerated that contradict what we say matters?

B. Where empathy has slipped into avoidance
1. Where am I holding back on clarity because I do not want to cause discomfort?
2. Whose circumstances do I regularly take into account without revisiting what still needs to be true?
3. Where have I adjusted expectations informally rather than discussing them explicitly?

4. What would the person concerned say they believe is expected of them right now?

5. If this pattern continues for another six months, who else will carry the cost?

C. On fairness, trust, and consistency

1. Do high performers in this organisation believe standards are applied fairly and consistently?

2. Where do people see a gap between what is said and what is actually tolerated?

3. How predictable are consequences when expectations are not met?

4. Would someone be genuinely surprised by negative feedback on their performance and if so, why?

5. What signals does our current approach to discipline send about what really matters here?

D. On the hidden costs of avoidance

1. Where is cognitive load increasing because expectations are unclear?

2. Which teams or individuals are quietly carrying additional work because others are not being addressed?

3. What noise has crept in (perhaps more reporting, more process, more meetings) as a substitute for clear early intervention?

4. Where has performance variability become person-dependent rather than system-reliable?

5. What are we normalising today that we would not have accepted two years ago?

E. On ownership and control

1. For our most critical outcomes, is ownership genuinely clear or is shared responsibility being used as cover for no responsibility?
2. Where are decision rights, escalation points, or accountability thresholds still ambiguous?
3. Who is responsible for intervening early when standards start to slip and do they know it?
4. How often are role responsibilities and KPIs meaningfully updated when structures or reporting lines change?
5. If something drifts significantly in the next three months, who will notice first and how?

Closing Reflection — Chapter 4

The leadership mistake I described at the opening of this chapter was not dramatic. It did not involve a single catastrophic decision or an obvious failure of judgement. It was a series of small, individually defensible choices; the decision to balance competing feedback rather than investigate it, to defer a direct conversation rather than have it, to choose the interpretation that required less of me in a moment that already felt over-full and challenging in greater ways.

That is precisely how discipline breaks down; not in a moment of weakness, but in a sequence of moments of entirely understandable, well-intentioned restraint and hesitation.

The cost of each individual deferral is almost always manageable, however the cost of all of them together rarely is.

*Here is a space for your own reflection on this chapter. What reso-
nated with you?*

(Write your thoughts here)

CHAPTER 5

ACCOUNTABILITY WITHOUT THE LANDMINES

"Effective leadership is putting first things first. Effective management is discipline, carrying it out."

—Stephen Covey,
Author, The 7 Habits of Highly Effective People

How to hold the line without destroying yourself in the process

When I boarded the plane to take on the role of President of our company's North American operations, just months after the world had been turned upside down by September 11, I had received exactly two pieces of guidance from my CEO.

The first came as a phone call the day before my departure where he articulated the mission: "Just don't f#%k it up."

Fabulous. No pressure. Message received loud and clear.

This was our third attempt at establishing a foothold in the North American market, and everyone in the organisation knew what that meant. Despite sustained investment in experienced people and serious resources across two previous attempts, we had not been able to figure it out. I had been told, in no uncertain terms, that if we did not succeed this time, there would not be a fourth attempt. I am certain that many Australian business leaders reading this will recognise that particular frontier. North America has a long and storied history of quietly defeating Australian businesses that arrived there with exceptional confidence and insufficient humility or acknowledgement of the market nuances. We were no different.

On a personal level, I was acutely aware of my own exposure. I had spent four years in a global executive HR role with indirect responsibility across seven countries, and I was proud of that work. But I was stepping out of a specialised functional role and directly into a high-pressure operational leadership position spanning two distinct and genuinely challenging international markets in USA and Canada. The company was taking a large bet on me. I did not want to let them down, and I was honest enough with myself to know that I was, in the most operational sense of the word, green.

The second instruction I received was rather more specific than the first.

I was expected, upon arrival, to rapidly terminate the employment of a particular country leader who had been reporting directly to the CEO for over five years and who had been a long-standing, valued member of the business across two continents. This outcome was presented to me as a fait accompli. A non-negotiable directive to be executed promptly.

My response, and I acknowledge this was perhaps not my most diplomatically refined moment, was to ask the CEO directly: "If this is what desperately needs to happen, why haven't *you* done it yourself in the five years this person has reported to you?"

Inappropriate directness, as I have mentioned before, is a known character flaw of mine. I make no apologies for it.

What emerged through the conversations that followed, before I departed, was a story I have since encountered in some form in virtually every organisation I have worked with across thirty years and multiple continents. During the preceding five years, there had been no definable performance management process or conversations applied to this individual. No difficult discussions either in passing or on record. No specific expectations ever laid out or documented. No timeframes for improvement given or discussed openly. No clarity provided about the gap between what was needed and what was being delivered.

This was not because the CEO was indifferent or unkind. The reasons were entirely understandable and the relationship was long-standing. The individual's prior contributions were real, the market was complex, and hope is a surprisingly persistent management strategy when the alternative feels both risky and unkind. But I have learned that understandable is not the same as defensible. And the consequences of that avoidance had been building quietly for years, until eventually they became my problem to solve at thirty thousand feet, en-route to a market I had never operated in, with a directive I had serious reservations about following.

I pushed back firmly. I told the CEO I wanted time to understand both the market and the individual, and I asked for the right to make my own decision at my own discretion. Despite repeated reminders of the original directive once I was on the ground (and believe me there were many) I held my position.

What followed over the next eight months shaped the way I think about accountability, performance, and human dignity in leadership more than almost any other experience in my career.

The conversations I was able to have with that leader – open, honest, direct, and conducted in the language of real humans rather than the stilted vocabulary of formal performance processes, had genuinely productive outcomes for both of us. I will not pretend it was easy to navigate for either of us. I am not sure that individual ever fully respected me, though I hope they understood that I respected them. What I gave them, and what had been previously withheld and without malicious intent, was clarity.

Clarity about the expectations, about the gaps, about what was working and what was not. Every day in our daily discussions around what we were immediately facing into, not in quarterly reviews. In real time, in real language, between two people who both genuinely cared about the outcome and the business.

Ultimately, it was appropriate that this person exited the business. That conversation happened, when it needed to, in a humane and empathetic way. From memory I shed more tears that day than the person exiting which was not surprising. I negotiated hard for a generous exit arrangement and achieved a better outcome for them than others in more senior positions had been able to achieve, and we all moved on with our dignity intact.

But here is what that experience crystallised for me, and it is the argument that underpins this entire chapter.

Authentic and effective performance management is not an event driven by "tick the box" theatre.

It is not the formal review, the written warning, or the performance improvement plan. It is how we show up for each other every single day: reinforcing expectations, addressing gaps in real time, supporting improvement as it happens, and having the courage to name what is not working before it calcifies into an irreversible problem.

Performance gaps reserved for infrequent, formal, emotionally charged discussions deny both parties the opportunity to actually change anything together. They transform what could be a collaborative regular conversation into an awkward crisis.

What I have seen, in organisation after organisation across thirty years, is that hope has become the dominant performance management strategy for too many leaders. There are many causal reasons for this that we will dive into shortly and it is costing dearly; the individual being managed, the team around them, and the organisation carrying the accumulated weight of the things that were never said and countless lost opportunities to build trust and gently deliver key messages in a consistent way.

This chapter will give you a better strategy than hope.

Why the modern workplace has made leaders afraid of their own authority

I want to be fair about how we arrived here, because the shift toward a more legally cautious, emotionally sensitive workplace did not happen arbitrarily. Many of the HR frameworks, employment protections, legislative and governance structures that now make accountability conversations feel so treacherous were introduced in direct response to genuine failures. We have all read about or experienced workplace bullying that was real and seriously damaging, performance processes weaponised to disguise discrimination, and power imbalances that left people with no recourse. That context matters, and I am not dismissing it.

But something has gone significantly wrong in the workplace translation, specifically in how it has impacted our ability to drive performance outcomes, accountability and discipline across leadership cohorts.

What began as a necessary and overdue recalibration has, in many organisations, mutated into a culture of such profound risk aversion that leaders are now genuinely afraid to give honest feedback, set non-negotiable standards, or hold people to the expectations that were agreed at the beginning of the employment relationship. In some organisations I work with, the HR function has effectively become a protective barrier for under-performance rather than the infrastructure for fair and constructive management of people to the benefit of ALL parties.

I have personally seen senior leaders told by their HR teams not to document performance concerns in writing because it "creates a paper trail." I have seen CEOs advised not to have direct conversations about inadequate work because it "might constitute adverse action." And I have seen board directors fail to address the single most significant risk to their organisation through poor CEO performance or standards, because the individual in question lodged a pre-emptive complaint or warning signal, and everyone became too frightened to act.

This is not HR or leadership doing their job well. This is risk aversion masquerading as people management necessity, and it is making organisations slower, more dysfunctional, less outcome driven and ultimately more legally exposed by the day. That last point is important, and I will return to it shortly, because the legal landscape has just shifted in a way that most leaders do not yet fully understand. The other unintended consequence is that it can sometimes elevate the people who whinge the most, do the least work, and who are generally malcontent or incompetent, into a position of power they should not be afforded when performance is being well managed.

The law just changed and not in the direction you think

As of late 2025, Australia now has nationally consistent psychosocial hazard regulations across every jurisdiction, in one of the most significant shifts in workplace health and safety law in decades. Similar frameworks have been progressively implemented across the United Kingdom under the Health and Safety at Work Act and the Management of Health and Safety at Work Regulations, across Canada under provincial occupational health and safety legislation, and through the EU's Framework Directive and its subsequent member-state implementations, which explicitly include psychological health as a protected workplace dimension. In the United States, while there is no single equivalent federal statute, the convergence of OSHA general duty obligations, evolving case law, and state-level legislation is creating a comparable operating environment for large employers.

In the Australian context specifically, the new framework places psychosocial hazards – which include workplace bullying, job demands, role ambiguity, and work-related stress – on exactly the same legal footing as physical safety risks. Employers must now proactively identify, assess, control, and review psychosocial risks using the same hierarchy of controls framework previously applied only to physical hazards. The Department of Defence has already been convicted under this framework (the first Commonwealth employer conviction of its kind) for failing to adequately manage psychosocial risks in its workforce.

Many astute leaders and board directors I have spoken with in the past six months have read these regulations and concluded, with genuine alarm, that they now have even less room to hold people accountable. That they are more exposed than before and that the already treacherous terrain of performance management has become even more dangerous.

I want to suggest the opposite is true, and I want to suggest it not as a matter of opinion but as a matter of legal fact.

The same legislation that creates liability for unreasonable or oppressive management behaviour also (and this is the part that is almost never discussed in HR overviews to board and management) creates liability for the ***absence*** of management behaviour. Chronic ambiguity about expectations is a psychosocial hazard. A high-performing bully whose behaviour is tolerated because they are commercially valuable is a psychosocial hazard for every person working around them. Persistent under-performance left unaddressed, creating ongoing uncertainty and frustration in the team absorbing its consequences, is a psychosocial hazard. An organisation in which standards are applied inconsistently, where some people are held to account and others are visibly not, creates exactly the conditions of low role clarity and perceived unfairness that these regulations are designed to prevent.

The legislation has not made accountability more dangerous. *It has made the sustained* **avoidance** *of accountability legally untenable for the first time.*

The critical legal distinction, in Australia and in most equivalent international frameworks, is the concept of *reasonable management action*. Performance management, the setting of clear expectations, the delivery of honest feedback, and the management of under-performance through documented and fair processes are all explicitly excluded from the definition of psychosocial hazards, ***provided they are conducted reasonably.*** What the law does not protect is management action that is capricious, inconsistent, humiliating, or designed to harm rather than improve. The difference between those two things is not difficult to identify. It is the difference between the conversations my CEO should have consistently had five years earlier; clear, fair, documented, and given with genuine opportunity to respond, and the directive I was handed on a plane, asking me to clean up the consequence of five years of hoping the problem would solve itself.

This distinction between oppressive management and reasonable management action also shows up clearly in performance research. Large-scale studies of performance systems find that employees are far more likely to see performance management as effective when it is experienced as procedurally fair: when expectations are clear, standards are applied consistently, and goals are explicitly linked to what the organisation is actually trying to achieve.

In one McKinsey analysis, 60 per cent of respondents who perceived their performance-management system as fair also rated it as effective, and the organisations that invested in clarity, coaching capability, and transparent linkage between KPIs and strategy saw measurable improvements in engagement and productivity.

For leaders operating in international contexts, the practical implication is the same regardless of jurisdiction: the legal risk, in almost every developed labour market, does not arise from managing people directly and fairly. It arises from managing them badly; inconsistently, without notice, without documentation, or for reasons unrelated to performance. Understanding that distinction is what transforms the accountability conversation from a legal minefield into straightforward professional leadership.

What the law actually requires (and what it does not)

I should pause and say that I am not a lawyer, and nothing in this section constitutes legal advice for your specific situation or jurisdiction. What I offer is an operational perspective built across many years of working inside and alongside organisations navigating these issues across multiple countries and legal environments.

With that clearly stated, here is what consistently surprises leaders when they actually engage with the legal framework rather than fearing it from a distance.

Employment law in Australia, the United Kingdom, Canada, and most comparable jurisdictions does not protect people from being managed. It protects people from being managed *unfairly* or improperly; without notice, inconsistently, for discriminatory reasons, or in a manner designed to demean rather than improve. That is a critically important distinction that changes the entire accountability conversation.

The legal risk, in the vast majority of cases, arises from these specific failures: holding someone accountable for standards that were never clearly communicated; applying expectations inconsistently across comparable situations; delivering feedback in a manner that is humiliating, threatening or personal rather than professional; conflating performance management with a protected attribute such as age, gender, disability, or cultural background; and (most commonly) taking consequential action without first giving the person a genuine and supported opportunity to respond and improve.

None of those failures are likely in a direct, honest, accountability conversation. They are all things a well-prepared leader can avoid without compromising the core message that needs to be delivered. When leaders understand this clearly, something important shifts. The conversation that felt dangerous starts to feel manageable. The question stops being *can* I have this conversation, and becomes *how* do I have it in a way that is both legally sound and humanly honest?

This is why having clarity on how to approach and effectively deliver these conversations is an even more critical part of our leadership tool kit moving forward.

Turns out the conversation everyone was dreading was also the one everyone needed.

The five conversations most leaders avoid and how to have them

In my experience, the accountability conversations that leaders most consistently avoid tend to cluster around five recognisable situations. Each has its own complexity, its own specific landmines, and its own practical approach that works better than the alternatives.

1. The underperforming long-tenured employee
This is the scenario I described from my North American experience, and it is the one I encounter most frequently. The individual has been in the organisation for a significant period of time. They are liked. Their historical contribution is real but something has shifted: their performance, their capability, their motivation, or the role and operating environment itself and the gap between what they are delivering and what is genuinely needed has been growing for months, sometimes years. Everyone around them recognises the issues and there are clear flow on impacts to the business, however no one has said it clearly to them.

The instinctive response is to wait for a better moment, hope things will improve, and give them the benefit of the doubt until the gap becomes so obvious that decisive and extreme intervention and action become unavoidable. By that point, the organisation has usually absorbed enormous cost (both real and opportunity), the individual's own confidence has quietly deteriorated without clear feedback, and any intervention now lands as punitive rather than constructive. The intervention is also, at that stage, far more legally exposed; precisely because there is no record of earlier, reasonable management action.

The approach that works begins with a direct, specific, and human conversation that names the gap without personalising it.

Not *"I am concerned about how things are going for you"* because that is too vague to act on.

Not *"your performance has been unacceptable"* because that is too broad to contest.

Something like: *"I want to have an honest conversation with you about [specific outcome or behaviour]. The standard we need here is [specific]. What I have observed over [specific time period] is [specific examples]. I want to understand your perspective, and I also want to be clear that this needs to change. Let us talk about what is getting in the way and what support looks like from my side."*

The craft is in delivering that with enough consistency, steadiness and enough genuine care that the person across the table feels held accountable but not discarded. That is the balance I was able to find in those eight months with that earlier example in North America. It is not always achievable, but it is always worth attempting.

Remember that *the more frequently you have these open and honest conversations, the more genuine opportunity you open up for change and growth to happen* instead of storing it up for an annual review.

2. The high-performer whose behaviour is unacceptable

This is, in many ways, more difficult than the first because the organisation's instinct is to protect someone it perceives as commercially or technically indispensable. I have worked with organisations where a brilliant individual has been allowed to bully, undermine, or exclude colleagues for years because the business could not afford to lose them, or convinced itself it could not. Make no mistake this happens as often at the CEO level as it does through the various ranks of the organisation. The damage done to everyone else during that period is almost never honestly reckoned with.

The principle here is non-negotiable and entirely straightforward: there is no performance outcome that licenses unacceptable behaviour. The moment an organisation makes that exception, it has communicated something to every single person watching (which is everyone) about who has to meet the standards of conduct and who does not. The psychosocial legislation makes this more than a cultural argument; it is now a legal one. Tolerating a high performer's harmful behaviour toward colleagues creates identifiable, documented psychosocial hazard liability for the organisation. The conversation is identical in structure to every other accountability conversation. The stakes for not having it have simply increased.

Accordingly, in this legislative context, boards are now on notice that actively and fairly managing CEO performance and dynamics is far more of a risk and necessity than ever before.

3. The conversation with someone who is genuinely struggling personally

From my own leadership experience, this is where empathy and accountability feel most sharply in tension, and where leaders most commonly lose their way; not through indifference, but through kindness taken too far. Someone is navigating a health crisis, a family breakdown, a bereavement or another genuinely distressing personal issue that is impacting their work and performance. The leader does not want to compound their distress and that instinct is empathetic, right and important.

What goes wrong is when *"I will give them some space"* extends silently for months, without any honest communication about expectations, until the situation eventually escalates into a formal performance or disciplinary process that the person genuinely did not see coming. Because no one had told them directly that the performance standard still applied during that period, or alternatively that they did not openly review and agree a new performance standard and outcomes for a defined period of time while they worked through their issues.

Empathy without clarity is not kindness. It is a delayed and significantly more painful form of harm. The approach that works separates two distinct conversations explicitly.

One is: *"I want to acknowledge what you are going through. Let us talk about what support and flexibility make sense from us during this period."* The second, held either simultaneously or very shortly after, is: *"I also want to be honest with you about what we need from this role, and what the minimum viable contribution looks like over the coming months. I want to make sure you have full clarity, so you are not carrying any additional professional uncertainty on top of everything else."*

Having both conversations, explicitly and separately, is the most genuinely supportive thing a leader can do for someone in that position. It removes the fog of ambiguity at a time when everything else is already uncertain.

4. The senior leader or peer whose performance needs addressing, but whose positional power makes the conversation feel politically dangerous

This is where abdication is most common and can apply equally to performance discussions between boards and CEOs as it does throughout other levels of the organisation. The person is too senior, too well-connected, or too entrenched for anyone to feel safe raising the issue directly. They have often been in the organisation long enough to know exactly how to activate their informal networks (both upwards and downwards) the moment they feel their position is threatened.

The framework here is identical: the behaviour or performance is named specifically, the standard is restated clearly, the expectation for change is made explicit. What changes is the preparation required beforehand and the escalation pathway you have thought through in advance.

Before this conversation, you need absolute clarity about your mandate and authority. You need to know who else is aware of the issue and where they stand. And you need to have genuinely worked through what you will do if the person responds by escalating politically rather than engaging professionally. Having thought through those scenarios before you walk in is what allows you to deliver the conversation with the quiet steadiness that makes it land and resonate, rather than the visible anxiety that invites a counter-offensive.

5. The conversation that follows an HR complaint or legal threat
In many ways this is often the hardest.

When someone has lodged a complaint or engaged representation, most leaders go into complete freeze. They stop all direct communication. They refer everything to HR or legal. And the underlying gap that existed before the complaint was made simply widens and hardens in silence.

In most complaint scenarios I have been involved in during my career, the escalation was made worse (more entrenched, more expensive, and more damaging to everyone involved) by the total withdrawal of direct, respectful leadership engagement. People who feel shut out after making a complaint become more determined, not less. There are specific situations where your legal counsel will rightly advise against direct contact, and you must follow that advice precisely.

But the default instinct to cease all human engagement is, in the majority of cases, strategically and humanly wrong and drives a huge wedge of distrust into the working relationship. People who are engaged with dignity, consistency, and clarity, even within the structure of a formal process, more often than not find a path through it.

The language that works and the language that makes it worse

One of the most practically useful things I can offer from decades of these conversations is the specific linguistic distinction between what opens a conversation and what closes it down.

Language that closes the conversation tends to be global rather than specific (*"your attitude has been a problem"*), retrospective without being constructive (*"this has been going on far too long"*), emotionally evaluative rather than factual (*"I have to tell you, I am really disappointed"*), or implicitly threatening without being explicit about consequence (*"this really cannot continue the way things are going"*).

Each of these patterns triggers the defensive response that makes genuine accountability impossible. The person stops listening to what is being said and starts composing their rebuttal.

Language that keeps the conversation open is: specific rather than global (*"on these specific occasions over the past three weeks, this is what I observed"*); forward-focused rather than retrospective (*"what I need to see change is this, specifically"*); factual rather than evaluative (*"the outcome here was X, and the standard we need is Y"*); and explicit about both expectation and consequence (*"if this does not change, here is what happens next"*).

That last element, which is explicit consequence, is the one that makes most leaders' hands sweat (even mine!), and it is the one that matters most. A performance conversation that does not clearly communicate what happens if nothing changes is not a performance conversation. It is a venting exercise dressed up as management. The person leaves the room not knowing whether they are in genuine trouble or whether their boss simply had a difficult morning. That ambiguity is not kind. It is an abdication of the most important part of your responsibility as a leader.

Naming consequence clearly does not mean delivering it with relish or severity. In North America, in those ongoing conversations with a leader I had been directed to terminate before I had even unpacked, I named the reality directly: that the business needed specific things from this role; that they were not currently happening; that the stakes were high for both of us; and that I needed to understand what was getting in the way.

The ensuing conversations which were frank, specific, and human, were also more respectful than anything a single formal performance process could have delivered. It gave that person something they had not been given in five years: the truth, in time to do something about it.

The documentation that protects everyone

Documentation is the area where leaders most commonly either over-engineer. They create formal paper trails (ably assisted by formal HR word-speak) that feel disproportionate and signal distrust, or conversely under-prepare, having critical conversations that leave no record at all and create a "he said, she said" vulnerability that helps no one if things escalate.

The principle I have found most useful across multiple countries and legal frameworks is this: document for the benefit of the person in front of you, not for your protection *from* them.

A brief, factual summary after a significant conversation; confirming what was discussed, what was agreed, and what the next steps are, is not a surveillance exercise. It is a service to each party. It ensures both parties are working from the same understanding, which is especially important in emotionally charged conversations where people hear selectively. It removes ambiguity about expectations. And it creates a record that, if things go well, is simply a marker of a constructive conversation. And if things do not, it demonstrates clearly that the individual was treated fairly and given every reasonable opportunity to respond.

The most effective framing I have observed being used is to close every significant accountability conversation with: *"I am going to send you a brief note summarising what we have discussed and what we have agreed. I want to make sure we are both working from exactly the same understanding."* That framing is collaborative, not adversarial. It invites the person to come back and say *"I understood it slightly differently"* which is often the most useful information you can receive, and which itself becomes part of the documented record of a fair and transparent process.

Why clarity is kinder than kindness

I want to close this chapter with the principle that I believe is most misunderstood in the entire discipline of people leadership.

In our increasingly well-intentioned effort to be kind we have often created a workplace culture in which people are routinely denied the one thing that would genuinely help them most: clear, honest, timely feedback about the gap between where they are and where they need to be and the support required to bridge that gap.

I have sat with people after they have been terminated from organisations they gave years of their working life to, and one of the most consistent things I hear is some version of: *"No one ever actually told me"* or *"I never saw that coming".*" Not in a way that felt real or that made the seriousness clear. Not in a way that gave them a genuine opportunity to respond and change.

That is not kindness. That is an extended and agonising postponement of the inevitable, made worse at every stage by the accumulated weight of the things that were never said.

The most respectful thing you can do for another professional, regardless of their level, their tenure, or the circumstances you find yourself navigating is tell them the truth about how they are performing, tell them clearly what needs to change, give them a real and genuinely supported opportunity to respond, and then follow through consistently on whatever you said would happen next. In many cases, that approach leads people to self-select themselves out of organisations with grace and ease because they understand clearly where the gaps exist and that the role or organisation is not the best fit for them. In my eyes, that is a brilliant outcome for all parties.

This is not just my personal philosophy. Research on leadership habits and self-discipline shows that small, consistent behaviours – weekly one-on-ones, regular feedback and predictable communication rhythms – all compound into measurable improvements in engagement, decision quality, retention, and innovation.

Leaders who treat these behaviours as optional extras or personality-dependent "good days" never see those gains. Leaders who turn them into non-negotiable habits effectively hard-wire discipline into the way their teams experience work every week.

That is what I was able to achieve to a large extent in North America, imperfectly and under pressure, with a leader who had been denied that basic professional courtesy for five years. It did not produce a fairytale outcome, they ultimately left the business, as perhaps they always were going to. But they left with dignity. They left knowing they had been seen clearly, treated honestly, and given every possible opportunity. And I left knowing I had led that process in a way I could stand behind instead of merely executing orders.

When accountability is delivered with that genuine intention and effort, it does not destroy cultures. It builds them.

People do not leave organisations where they are held to clear, fair, consistent standards by leaders who genuinely care about their development and their dignity. They leave organisations where they are either ignored until things become critical, or managed through a system so weighted toward avoidance that they never really know where they stand.

Accountability, delivered well, is not the opposite of a great workplace culture.

This is the Discipline Dividend at its most human; earned not in a single decision but in the accumulated weight of a thousand smaller ones and the lived experience of an organisation in which people know where they stand, trust that the standard applies to everyone equally, and are genuinely set up to succeed rather than quietly managed toward an exit they never saw coming.

It *is* a great workplace culture.

TOOLBOX — Chapter 5

Practical questions and frameworks for accountability conversations

Use these to prepare for the conversations that matter; not as a checklist for every minor interaction, but for the ones you have been avoiding, the ones you know need to happen, and the ones where the stakes are high enough that doing it well (or badly) will leave a mark.

A. Preparing for the conversation

1. What specific outcome, behaviour, or performance gap am I addressing, and can I describe it with concrete examples rather than general patterns?
2. Was the standard I am holding this person to clearly communicated beforehand, or am I introducing it for the first time in this conversation?
3. Have I applied this standard consistently to others in comparable situations, or could this person reasonably argue they are being treated differently?
4. What outcome do I genuinely want from this conversation? Improvement, a reset, or a managed exit and am I being honest with myself about which one I am actually pursuing?
5. What specific support am I prepared to offer, and have I thought that through concretely?

B. Checking your own position

1. Am I having this conversation because it is the right time, or because I have finally run out of road on avoiding it?

2. Have I been sufficiently direct in previous conversations, or has this person received mixed signals about how serious the situation is?

3. Am I addressing this person's performance, or am I actually addressing a role, structure, or systemic issue that I am attributing to an individual?

4. What is my emotional state going into this, and is any part of my preparation about managing my own discomfort rather than serving the other person?

5. If this person's closest colleague asked them tomorrow what happened in this meeting, what would I want them to honestly be able to say?

C. Language and delivery

1. Have I described specific behaviour and outcomes, or have I described my emotional response to them?

2. Have I named the standard clearly enough that this person knows exactly what "better" looks like?

3. Have I been explicit about consequence; not implied or hinted, but directly stated?

4. Have I created enough space for the other person to genuinely respond, or have I structured this as a monologue?

5. How will I respond if they cry, get angry, threaten HR, or go completely silent?

D. Documentation and follow-through

1. What summary will I send after this conversation, and how will I frame it as a shared record rather than an adversarial one?

2. What are the specific next steps, specifically timeframes, check-in points, and clear markers of what constitutes genuine improvement?

3. Who else needs to be aware of this conversation, and how and when will I communicate that?

4. What is the specific trigger that tells me improvement has been sufficient and what is the trigger that tells me I need to move to the next stage?

5. Am I prepared to follow through on the consequence I named, or have I set an expectation I will not actually honour?

E. After the conversation

1. Did I say what I intended, or did I soften it in the moment in a way that may have undermined the message?

2. Does this person leave knowing exactly where they stand and what is expected of them?

3. Did I listen as well as I spoke and did anything they said change my understanding of the situation?

4. Is there anything in how I handled this that I would do differently?

5. What support does this person now need; not to be shielded from accountability, but to be genuinely set up to succeed against the standard?

Closing Reflection — Chapter 5

The accountability conversation you are avoiding is not protecting the person in front of you.

It is protecting you from your own discomfort while they continue working in a fog of uncommunicated expectations and unaddressed gaps.

The most generous, professional, and legally sound thing you can do is say it clearly, say it early, and mean it when you do.

Clarity is not cruelty, however avoidance is.

Here is a space for your own reflection on this chapter. What resonated with you?

(Write your thoughts here)

____

____

____

____

____

CHAPTER 6

THE JUDGEMENT GAP: WHY DECISIONS ARE GETTING WORSE

"It's only when the tide goes out that you discover who's been swimming naked."

—Warren Buffett,
Chairman and CEO, Berkshire Hathaway

One of the privileges (and occasional penalties) of a career that has spanned executive, C-suite, advisory, and board roles is that you accumulate a front-row seat to an enormous range of human decision-making. The brilliant calls made under impossible pressure. The catastrophic ones made in rooms full of intelligent, experienced people who, by any reasonable measure, should have known better. And the myriad of ones that sit in the uncomfortable "messy" middle: not dramatic failures, just a slow, compounding erosion of judgement that nobody quite notices until the damage is already done.

There is a moment I have watched play out, in different forms, in boardrooms and executive team meetings across multiple industries. It is the specific moment when someone in the room knows that the trajectory is wrong, that the story being told does not match the data being produced, and that a decision based on the prevailing narrative is going to produce an outcome that will later feel entirely avoidable. And they say nothing. Not because they lack courage, or are indifferent. But because the social architecture of the room has made saying the truth feel more professionally dangerous than allowing the comfortable version to go unchallenged.

That moment, and the accumulation of those moments, is what this chapter is about.

Over the years I have been fortunate to build a network of professionals I genuinely trust. These are people who have supported me through my own career challenges as generously as I have tried to support them through theirs. One of these friends held a C-suite role in an exceptionally successful, intergenerational niche infrastructure business. From the sidelines, I watched that business go off the rails; in hindsight both predictably and unnecessarily, with consequences that were devastating for the people involved. I want to be clear upfront: this story does not have a happy ending.

The company was led by a young CEO, Peter, who was the child of the founder. Despite growing up around the business, he had studied and worked externally with a credible organisation before stepping back into the company in the top role, in line with a carefully considered succession plan. Peter was dynamic and undeniably charismatic. Intelligent and genuinely talented. Keen to make his mark in the family business, he delivered an exciting new growth strategy that was duly agreed and signed off by the board. The strategy involved what appeared, on the surface, to be a relatively subtle shift in target demographic. The intent was to build a significantly larger and more profitable customer base by aggressively pursuing adjacent segments to the company's core offering.

The costs of implementing that strategy were high, both organically and through a series of targeted, large-scale acquisitions. But commitment to it at every level of the organisation, from the CEO, the board, to the broader leadership team and business was strong.

Until it wasn't.

Rapidly acquired businesses failed to deliver their profitability forecasts. Cash positions weakened and debt grew. Customers stopped renewing service contracts, citing service failures. New customer acquisition stalled. Internally, resources became strained, executive attention remained relentlessly focused on the next acquisition target rather than on the integration failures that were quietly undermining the foundations of everything already in place. Bringing in additional resources compounded head office costs and new hires underperformed due to insufficient on-boarding and development.

Despite a deteriorating cash position and falling profitability, the acquisitions continued into years two and three, still driven by the revenue growth targets embedded in the original strategy.

You have probably already anticipated where this ends. The business finally fell into administration. Jobs were lost and careers were damaged. Years of carefully built professional and personal credibility, on both sides of the board table, did not survive the outcome intact.

When I sat with my friend afterwards, while they were still processing the professional and personal aftermath of an extraordinarily stressful period, I asked them how it had been allowed to go so far, so far past the point where the evidence was unambiguous. The explanation was not one of ignorance or bad intent. It was something far more common and far more instructive than either of those things.

The warning signs had been coming from multiple directions for a long time. Everyone with eyes close enough to the numbers could see them. And quite simply, nobody acted.

The CEO Peter was so charismatic and persuasive, and so skilled at leveraging both familial and personal relationships on the board, that they were consistently able to buy more time for the plan to succeed, long past the point where the data justified that patience. His reputation from his previous external role carried more weight in the boardroom than the quantitative reality sitting in front of the directors, who consistently believed their CEO knew what he was doing and would find a way to get it right. There was an elevated desire and belief that Peter would succeed and take the family business to the next level, and it was difficult to broach the subject of CEO performance with the founder Chair given the family relationship.

The information flowing to the board had become increasingly curated: externally attributing causes for under-performance, shifting the emphasis of key metrics over time, and lacking the credible consistency and accuracy that independent directors are supposed to demand and receive. And the board itself, which was composed predominantly of long-standing friends of the founder, many of whom had sat together around that table (and at that family's kitchen table) for more than a decade, had neither the composition, the inclination or (quite frankly) the kahunas to deliver the accountability, interrogation, or governance rigour the situation required.

The final ingredient, and in my experience, always the one that makes the difference between a problem identified in time and a catastrophe, was the absence of agreed strategic measures, consistently monitored, transparently reported, and meaningfully linked to timeframes and consequences. Without those anchors, strategic drift not only continues well past the point of intervention; it becomes almost impossible for anyone in the room to make the definitive case that the moment for action has arrived.

I have seen too many variations of this story to count them. And I want to be direct about something that often gets lost in the telling of these cases: this is not purely a family business or small private company phenomenon. The same contributing factors: narrative dominance, board composition and inertia, metric drift, and the weight of a charismatic leader's reputation and "likeability" overriding uncomfortable evidence, similarly show up around the tables of ASX-listed companies with the same frequency, and with consequences that are equally serious for the people caught inside them.

What looks, in hindsight, like a single catastrophic failure is almost always a series of smaller, apparently independent decisions that compound over time into an outcome nobody consciously chose. That is precisely what makes the judgement gap so dangerous. It does not announce itself. It accumulates.

Why good judgement Is eroding in rooms full of smart people

The question I am most frequently asked when I describe situations like the one above is some version of "how does this happen?" These are not stupid or careless people. They are, in many cases, deeply experienced professionals who have navigated significant complexity before in their distinguished careers. How does a boardroom full of capable directors watch a business march confidently towards peril and not intervene?

The answer is not a single failure. It is a predictable convergence of several dynamics that individually appear manageable but together become disabling. And once you can see them clearly and know what you are looking at, you typically begin to recognise them everywhere. In strategy meetings. In executive teams. In your own decision-making on a pressured Tuesday afternoon.

Understanding those dynamics is what this chapter is about.

The narrative trap

The most powerful force acting against good judgement in any organisation is not bad data, inadequate process, or even insufficient experience. It is a compelling narrative, delivered confidently by capable individuals, that has stopped being tested and validated.

Every organisation runs on narrative. It is how complexity gets simplified into something manageable, how strategy gets communicated, how leaders build the alignment they need to move large groups of people in a shared direction. Informal "around the water cooler" narratives shape culture. Narrative is not inherently problematic. However, it becomes dangerous at precisely the point when it transitions from a working hypothesis about the world into an unquestionable truth. When the story the organisation tells about itself, its market, and its strategy becomes more persuasive than the evidence that might challenge it.

In the case I described above, the narrative was entirely coherent and genuinely compelling: a talented new CEO; external credibility; a well-considered growth strategy; a board with deep knowledge of the business and the family. That narrative was not wrong when the strategy was conceived. It became dangerous when it continued to carry more evidential weight than the cash flow statements, the missing data points in board reports, the customer churn data, and the integration failures that were accumulating in plain sight.

This is what I mean by the judgement gap. It is not the gap between what leaders know and what they decide. It is the gap between what the evidence says (when the right and complete set of information is consistently presented clearly and openly) and what the prevailing narrative allows people to hear. When that gap exists and is not challenged, decision quality degrades. Not because the people in the room are intellectually incapable of seeing the problem, but because the organisational and relational dynamics make seeing it, naming it, and acting on it feel more challenging and dangerous than continuing to believe.

The five dynamics that corrupt decision quality

Across executive teams, boardrooms, and advisory engagements, I have observed that the corruption of good judgement almost always involves some combination of five recognisable dynamics which rarely arrive alone.

1. Authority and influence substituting for evidence

When the most senior, most credible, or most charismatic person in the room has a clear position, the quality of the decision that follows depends almost entirely on whether anyone else in that room is genuinely prepared to challenge it. In most organisations, the answer in practice rather than in theory unfortunately is no.

Not from indifference, but from the entirely rational calculation that challenging the CEO or the dominant board voice carries personal and professional risk that agreeing does not.

Research on board decision-making is unambiguous on this point: in rooms where hierarchy and confidence dominate, dissent is suppressed, assumptions go untested, and the quality of final decisions is systematically lower than the collective capability of the people in the room would suggest. The business I described above did not fail because its board lacked intelligence or experience. It failed because the authority of one individual, amplified by personal relationships, succession narrative, and prior reputation, was consistently allowed to substitute for the inconvenient evidence that was available throughout.

I have sat in enough of those rooms to know how powerful that dynamic is from the inside. The CEO presents with absolute conviction. The numbers are explained, credibly and articulately, as temporary, external, or already being addressed. The room *really* wants to believe it. And the person who would need to say *"I do not think that is right, and here is why"* makes a quiet, almost unconscious calculation about what that moment will cost them, be that relationally, politically, or professionally, and decides to let that moment pass.

Multiply that calculation across a two-year period and across a boardroom of twelve people, and you have a board acting more as box-tickers and administrators than guardians of strategy and outcomes.

2. Metric drift

One of the subtlest and most reliably damaging patterns I observe in organisations is the gradual, often unconscious migration of reported metrics away from the ones that would most clearly signal a problem. It rarely happens through deliberate deception (although sometimes worryingly it does). More commonly it happens through the entirely human instinct to emphasise what is going well and down-play and contextualise what is not.

Over time, the metrics that appear in board papers begin to reflect the story that *management wants to tell* rather than the story the *business* actually needs the board to hear. KPIs that were agreed at the outset of a strategy quietly drop off the reporting deck and are replaced by measures that are trending more favourably. Targets are retrospectively adjusted without formal discussion and are often accompanied by vague narratives about the elements that are outside management control. Comparative benchmarks shift and trend analysis becomes less prominent, or is often fully missing from both metrics and commentary. The board, receiving a curated version of operational reality, makes decisions based on a dataset that has been highly filtered through the very management team whose performance it is supposed to be assessing and holding to account.

The antidote to metric drift is not more metrics. It is fewer, better ones agreed before the strategy is implemented, linked explicitly to timeframes and consequences, owned by specific individuals, and reviewed by people with genuine independence from the management narrative. That is a governance discipline, not a management one. And it is one that boards consistently pause to reflect on and underinvest in, to their considerable cost.

3. Relationship inertia on boards

Long-standing boards with deep relationships are often in reality, a specific and underappreciated governance risk. The familiarity that accumulates across a decade or more of shared table, whether a boardroom table or, as in the case above, also a kitchen table can too often create relational dynamics that are directly corrosive to independent judgement. Directors who have known each other, and known the management team, for years find it progressively more difficult to ask the question that most needs asking, because the social cost of doing so has become entangled with relationships they value.

The governance literature on this is consistent and sobering. Boards that have not renewed their composition meaningfully – in skills, perspective, industry currency, and personal independence from management – are demonstrably less likely to challenge under-performance or question strategic assumptions, and more likely to defer to management narratives past the point at which the evidence justifies that deference. The Australian Institute of Company Directors (AICD) has made board renewal a governance priority precisely because the research on the cost of composition inertia is so clear.

I am not suggesting that experience and continuity on a board have no value because undoubtedly, they do. The board members who understand a business's history, culture, and competitive context most deeply are often its most valuable governors and can be its best ambassadors, providing continuity and context which is crucial to underpin strategy and assure external markets of continuity. The problem is not tenure. It is the absence of robust and deliberate independent challenge that tenure, when unaccompanied by diversity and renewal, tends to produce.

4. The confusion of confidence with competence

One of the most persistent and damaging misreadings in leadership is the equation of decisive, articulate confidence with deep, tested judgement. They are not the same thing, in fact they are not even reliably correlated. But in most organisational and governance cultures, they are treated as synonymous, and the consequences of that misreading show up with remarkable consistency in post-mortems on strategic failures.

In the case above, the CEO's confidence and charisma, grounded in genuine ability, genuine prior achievement, and genuine commitment to their strategy and the family legacy, was read by the board as evidence that the strategy was sound. To be clear, it was not evidence of that; it was evidence that the CEO believed it was sound and those are very different things. A board doing its job properly understands the difference.

I have worked with many leaders who were exceptionally confident and largely right. I have worked with just as many who were exceptionally confident and very significantly wrong. The variable that distinguished the quality of their decision-making was not confidence; it was whether they consistently sought challenge before their positions hardened, and whether they were willing to treat their own convictions as hypotheses to be tested rather than conclusions to be defended and protected at all costs.

That discipline is far rarer than it should be, and it becomes rarer the more senior, successful, and institutionally unchallenged a leader becomes.

5. The absence of a single person in the room whose explicit role is to disagree

In every room where important decisions are made, there can often be a default toward agreement. People want to move forward and typically they want expedited alignment and consensus. They are aware of the social and political cost of being the persistent dissenter. In my experience, playing the role of the persistent, and somewhat annoyingly constant "challenger" to decisions and approaches, quite frankly becomes exhausting when the path of least resistance is almost always inevitably the one the room consistently takes.

This path is not weakness and it is important to recognise that it is entirely rational social behaviour in organisations that have not designed explicitly against it. High-reliability industries like aviation, nuclear, and emergency medicine, understood this decades ago and built structured dissent into their operating models at every level. The reason those industries have dramatically lower catastrophic failure rates than their risk profiles would otherwise predict is not that their people are smarter or more capable. It is that they have designed the conditions under which good judgement is possible, rather than assuming it will emerge naturally from a room of intelligent professionals.

What AI reveals and what it cannot fix

There is a reason this chapter sits at the intersection of the accountability argument and the AI argument in this book. The five dynamics I have just described: narrative dominance, metric drift, relationship inertia, the confusion of confidence with competence, and the absence of structural dissent are precisely the patterns that AI is now capable of surfacing in organisations, often before the humans in the room have registered that anything is wrong.

When pointed in the right direction, AI-enabled analytics can track metric drift across reporting periods and flag when the indicators in management reports have shifted materially from those agreed at the outset of a strategy. AI language analysis can identify when executive communications are increasingly externalising reasons for under-performance instead of accepting what they are actually in control of. Predictive modelling can surface the early signals of customer churn and cash deterioration months before they reach the severity that triggers board discussion. In the personal case study above, several of those signals were available in the data throughout the period of strategic drift. The problem was not data scarcity. It was the absence of the analytical infrastructure, and the cultural permission, to surface what the data was saying in a room where the prevailing narrative made it unwelcome and unpalatable to raise.

This is the most important thing I can say about AI and organisational decision-making in this incredibly fast-evolving AI landscape: AI does not create good judgement in organisations that have dismantled the conditions for it. What it does – which is both its value and its threat depending on the culture it is introduced into – is make poor judgement harder to hide. The narrative that has been substituting for evidence becomes far more identifiable and visible. The metric drift I spoke of earlier, becomes documentable. The gap between what the executive team is saying and what the operational data is showing becomes, for the first time, genuinely difficult and more uncomfortable to paper over.

For leaders who have been operating with discipline and integrity, I believe that transparency is a huge competitive advantage. For those who have been coasting on narrative, charm, and the accumulated goodwill of long-standing relationships, it is a reckoning that is coming regardless of whether they are ready for it.

We will return to this argument in detail in Chapter 7. For now, the relevant point is this: the judgement gap described in this chapter is not a problem that AI solves. It is a problem that human beings, operating in well-designed organisations with the courage to challenge their own narratives, must solve. AI can help us all to illuminate the gap, however it cannot close it.

What disciplined judgement actually looks like in practice

Disciplined judgement isn't about having all the facts.
It's about knowing when you have enough of them.

This chapter is not just about what I see going wrong, because good organisational judgement, while less dramatic than the failures, is equally observable in practice.

The organisations I have worked with that consistently make better decisions share a small number of characteristics that have nothing to do with the intelligence or experience of the individuals involved, and everything to do with the conditions those individuals operate within.

In these cases, they are explicitly, culturally and organisationally comfortable about what they *do not know*. In the best decision-making environments I have observed, it is entirely normal, even valued, for a senior leader to say *"I am not confident about this assumption, and here is why"* before a major decision is made. That willingness to name uncertainty before it becomes a crisis is one of the most reliable early indicators of organisational health I know. It is also, in most organisations, one of the rarest behaviours, especially at the board table where a lack of certainty by management can potentially be perceived as a flaw rather than a strength.

In these somewhat rare organisational examples, they clearly separate the *decision* from the *relationship.* In family businesses, founder-led organisations, and in fact in any environment where professional relationships are deeply entwined with personal ones, the ability to assess a leader's performance independently of your affection for them is genuinely difficult. On reflection, I have failed at this myself on occasion as indicated by the case study at the start of this Chapter.

The organisations that do it well have usually invested deliberately in structural mechanisms, independent directors, external advisors or third-party reviews to deliver true independent perspective, that create enough distance between the relationship and the assessment to allow honest evaluation to occur.

They review decisions for process *quality* and they value and emphasise this highly, not just outcome quality. One of the most damaging habits in organisational decision-making is the conflation of a good outcome with a good decision. A well-made decision can also produce a poor outcome: market conditions change, execution fails, assumptions that were reasonable at the time prove incorrect. Alternatively, a poorly made decision can combine with luck to get a good outcome.

I have witnessed that the organisations that improve their decision quality over time are the ones that examine *how* decisions were made: specifically what was assumed, what was challenged and what was ignored, rather than simply scoring the final result.

They treat strategic metrics as governance instruments, not management reports. The difference between a KPI dashboard that sits in an executive presentation and one that drives board-level accountability is not the data it contains. It is whether anyone around the table has agreed in advance what they will actually *do* when a specific indicator moves in a specific direction, and whether there are consequences; real, timely, and proportionate when those commitments are not met. In the case above, the absence of that agreement allowed strategic drift to compound across three years. It does not need to. But it requires a level of governance discipline that many boards, comfortable in long-standing relationships and trusting management implicitly, choose not to exercise until it is too late.

The question that changes everything

In thirty years of working alongside leaders and boards navigating complex, decisions, I have found that the single most valuable intervention available in any decision-making environment is also the simplest one.

It is asking, before the narrative settles:

"What would need to be true for us to be wrong about this?"

Not as a rhetorical exercise or as a token gesture toward intellectual rigour. But as a genuinely curious, unhurried, structurally protected question that the most senior person in the room is required to engage with honestly before the decision is committed to.

When approached in this manner, I see that answering this question does not, as some may assume, slow organisations down. It prevents acceleration in the wrong direction that is more expensive, disruptive, potentially humbling and time-consuming – both from an energy and resource perspective – to reverse than it would have been to avoid. It is the question that a well-composed, genuinely independent board should have been asking the CEO in the case I described above, from the first quarter in which the acquisition performance diverged from the forecast.

In this example, it was not asked. And a great many people paid the price of that silence.

I tell this story not to assign blame; the individuals involved were, in their different ways, doing what they believed was right, but because it is one of the most instructive examples I have witnessed of what happens when the conditions for good judgement are absent, and when the gap between what the evidence says and what the narrative allows is left to compound, quietly and eventually, fatally, across time.

The judgement gap is not inevitable. It is a design failure and like all design failures, it can be addressed; but only by leaders who are willing to examine their own decision-making environment with the same honesty they would bring to any other significant organisational risk.

TOOLBOX — Chapter 6

Questions to examine how decisions are actually being made in your organisation

Use these questions in your own reflection, with your leadership team, or as the basis for a genuine governance conversation. The most important ones are the ones that feel most uncomfortable to ask.

A. On narrative and evidence

1. What is the dominant narrative in my organisation right now about our strategy, our performance, or our direction and when was it last genuinely challenged?
2. Is there data available to me that, if I engaged with it honestly, would complicate or contradict the current narrative?
3. Who in my organisation has most clearly been signalling concern and how have those signals been received?
4. What would I need to believe to be true for our current strategy to be correct, and how confident am I that those beliefs are grounded in evidence rather than hope?
5. If I were an outsider looking at this organisation for the first time, what would the data tell me that the narrative is currently obscuring?

B. On authority and challenge

1. In the last significant decision made in my organisation, whose voice carried the most weight and was that weight proportional to the quality of the evidence they brought, or to their position and relationships?

2. Who in my team or on my board is genuinely prepared to challenge the dominant view and when did they last do so?

3. Have I made it structurally safe for people to disagree with me before decisions are made, or have I created conditions in which disagreement is theoretically welcome but practically career-limiting?

4. What decision have I made in the last twelve months that I am least confident about and how much genuine challenge did I invite before I committed to it?

5. If the most junior person with relevant knowledge in my organisation could speak freely about this decision, what would they say and how do we value that feedback?

C. On metrics and governance

1. Are the strategic metrics I am currently reporting the same ones that were agreed at the outset of this strategy and if not, what changed and why?

2. Do the people responsible for governing this organisation have access to the data that would most clearly signal a problem, or do they receive the data that management has determined they need?

3. For each of our key strategic commitments, is there a clearly agreed trigger that is specific, measurable, and time-bound that will initiate a formal review of whether the strategy remains sound?

4. Are there consequences attached to the failure to meet our strategic commitments, and are those consequences real and proportionate?

5. How long has it been since someone in a position of authority said, clearly and without qualification, that something significant is not working?

D. On board and leadership composition

1. Does my board or leadership team contain people whose primary qualification for being there is their relationship with the founder, the incumbent, or the dominant power and if so, what does that mean for the quality of challenge available?
2. When did my board or leadership team last have a genuinely uncomfortable conversation about under-performance – one that was not initiated by a crisis?
3. Is there diversity of perspective, industry experience, and genuine independence around my decision-making table or have I surrounded myself with people who are likely to agree?
4. What is the relational cost, in my current environment, of being the person who names the thing nobody wants to name and is that cost reasonable?
5. If this organisation were reviewed in three years and found to have made a series of poor decisions, which of the dynamics described in this chapter would the review most likely identify?

Closing Reflection — Chapter 6

Every significant organisational failure I have observed had a moment, sometimes many moments, when the evidence was available, someone in the room could see it or observe the absence of it, and the decision was made, consciously or not, not to act on it.

The judgement gap is not a gap in intelligence or experience.

It is a gap between what organisations know and what they are structurally, culturally, and relationally able to act on.

Closing that gap does not require extraordinary courage. It requires ordinary discipline, applied consistently, before the narrative becomes too expensive to challenge.

The judgement gap is, in this sense, the inverse of the Discipline Dividend. Where consistent analytical discipline pays compound returns in decision quality, its absence compounds in the opposite direction.

Each untested narrative, each unchallenged assumption, each deferred governance question adding quietly to an accumulating liability that eventually arrives as a crisis no one saw coming, despite the evidence that had been available throughout.

Here is a space for your own reflection on this chapter. What resonated with you?

(Write your thoughts here)

CHAPTER 7

WHAT AI SEES THAT YOU CANNOT

"The first rule of any technology used in a business is that automation applied to an efficient operation will magnify the efficiency. The second is that automation applied to an inefficient operation will magnify the inefficiency."

—Bill Gates,
co-founder, Microsoft

It's not that you weren't looking.
It's just that AI never blinks.

As I have sat around board tables and worked with organisations over the past twelve months, one thing has become increasingly and undeniably clear to me: AI is not a fad, and it is not another of those trends that disproportionately grabs our collective attention for a short, intense period before quietly fading into obscurity.

I can already hear a valid question forming in your mind: what makes me so certain in that assertion, given that I am definitely not a futurist? Quite simply, it is based on both my own experience of diving into that world with cautious curiosity and then, as time went on, somewhat headfirst, combined with the speed and breadth of application with which I am seeing AI being embedded into agile organisations, with profound and quantifiable commercial impact.

As I have already mentioned, this time last year my personal AI knowledge was astoundingly superficial and largely limited to what I was consuming in media, as opposed to being rooted in any meaningful practical experience. And based on what I was reading at the time, I will honestly admit that I was initially far more scared than curious, and it took me a considerably long time to properly dip my toes into the water.

I did this in the usual ways most of us "non-technical" people do: using ChatGPT as somewhat of an alternative to a Google search, making inanely simple and (in retrospect) embarrassingly generic requests, and consequently receiving generic answers that reflected precisely the basic, non-contextualised level of the prompt I had given it. Not surprisingly, the outputs were of limited professional use.

It was a shaky start. However, in conjunction with the learning that comes from repeated independent practice, I also made a deliberate decision that I needed to learn more from those who knew considerably more than me. In practice, that meant barely a week went by when I was not devouring videos, podcasts, in-person and online training sessions conducted by people who were applying AI in genuinely new and exciting professional contexts, and actively connecting with experts to stay updated on their thinking and work.

As with so many things in life, the more I used it, applied my growing knowledge, and deepened my understanding, the more confident I became in what I was producing with AI. I quickly noticed that when I applied elements of that newly-learned knowledge to the way I was interacting and prompting, the outputs I was receiving were significantly better each time, and the improvement was not incremental but genuinely step-changing in its quality and usefulness. I began to see AI tools as an incredibly capable thinking partner instead of an outsourced total solution, and by using it more thoughtfully and deliberately, I had a "super-power" at the end of my fingers.

I then started practically exploring the various large language models (LLMs) and the user experiences that each seemed to be better suited to, as they continued to evolve at an increasingly rapid rate. Before long, I was moving fluently between the various LLMs for different functions and purposes, and starting to get seriously impressed by what was becoming possible.

The real step change came when, on the back of the practical knowledge and the current and future use cases I was progressively uncovering, I made the decision to start a new business. Taking a structured approach and using AI tools throughout the entire process to help me identify, challenge, and refine the concept from initial thinking right through to deep consumer and customer research, counter-arguing against my own assumptions, working through potential business models and financial scenarios right through to drafting content and website development, I was quite frankly blown away by what I was able to achieve in an incredibly short timeframe. The confidence that process gave me to take the leap and begin the journey of building out my business, Illumetis, would simply never have happened at that pace or within those resources before. The barriers to getting to the starting gate had historically been high and costly, as they relied almost exclusively on human engagement and expertise for every element of that process.

Simultaneously, at a professional level, many of the businesses I work alongside day-to-day were beginning to seriously engage and move quickly on leveraging AI tools to drive quite dramatic improvements in process efficiency and quantifiable commercial outcomes. Once the genie was out of the bottle, it was very hard to get it back in, and I genuinely question why, at a corporate and commercial level, you would want to.

I do not for one second pretend that my AI knowledge is at an expert level. However, I continue to learn and grow it every day and remain genuinely excited about the opportunities we have to weave and integrate real, lived human experience and expertise around the extraordinary access to world-class knowledge that AI tools give us. The ability to find better ways to contextualise and leverage practical human insights into our AI outputs is, from my perspective, a genuinely powerful win win solution, and it is the problem I am determined to contribute to through my new business. But I am getting ahead of myself, and we will return to that in Chapter 11.

What I want to explore in this chapter is the broader AI leadership argument, because it goes significantly beyond any individual's personal adoption journey and reaches directly into the governance and decision-making dynamics we examined in the previous chapter.

Why AI changes the stakes for every leader in the room

The argument I made in Chapter 6 was that the judgement gap in organisations, specifically the corrosive distance between what the evidence shows and what the prevailing narrative allows people to hear, is not a new problem. It is, however, a worsening one, and one that has been allowed to compound because the conditions that once made it visible have gradually eroded. The dynamic I described in the infrastructure business that went into administration was not unusual. It was unfortunately typical. And the reason it was able to continue for as long as it did was not that the data was absent or that the people around the table were incapable; it was that the narrative was compelling enough, the relationships were close enough, and the cultural permission to challenge was so weak that the gap between evidence and decision remained invisible until it became catastrophic.

My observation is that AI changes that equation in ways that most organisations have not yet fully reckoned with, and that most leadership books have not yet caught up with.

The pattern-recognition capability of AI-enabled analytics is now sophisticated enough to identify the early signals of metric drift, narrative distortion, and performance deterioration months before those signals would register in a traditional governance review.

Automated agentic AI systems that monitor the consistency and accuracy of management reporting over time can detect when the metrics being reported to a board have shifted away from those agreed at the outset of a strategy, and can flag that shift without the political calculation that makes a human observer hesitate before raising the same concern.

Natural language AI processing tools can identify when executive reports are increasingly attributing under-performance to external factors, charting the linguistic drift from accountability to contextualisation in ways that no individual board director sitting in a quarterly meeting can easily observe. The financial and operational data that organisations already collect – artifacts like customer retention trends, margin movements, workforce signals – often contain a clear early warning of the trajectory that eventually ends in the kind of crisis I described in Chapter 6. AI can surface those signals with a consistency and absence of relational bias that human governance structures simply cannot replicate.

What this means in practice is important: in an AI-enabled governance environment, the quality of management information reaching a board is no longer primarily a function of what management chooses to present. It is increasingly a function of what the data independently reveals when interrogated by tools that have no interest in protecting the narrative, no relationship with the CEO, and no discomfort with asking the uncomfortable question for the fourteenth consecutive quarter.

At the time of writing this, I am yet to witness a board pro-actively and deliberately review all of their management reporting and data to identify where the opportunity lies to re-calibrate management reporting optimising for AI analysis. However, I do not feel that is far away for all of us.

For leaders and boards who have been operating with genuine transparency and discipline, this is an almost entirely positive development because it strengthens the architecture that supports good decision-making and reduces the cognitive load of detecting problems early. For those who have been relying, consciously or otherwise, on the natural human reluctance to challenge a compelling narrative from a trusted and credentialled source, it is a materially different proposition.

What AI cannot see and why that is where experience becomes decisive

I am not making the argument that AI replaces human judgement. It is almost the opposite of that, and the distinction matters enormously in how senior leaders position themselves in relation to these tools.

AI is extraordinarily good at detecting patterns in structured data, surfacing anomalies across large and complex datasets, processing information at a speed and scale that far exceeds human capacity, and doing all of that without the motivational distortions that affect human judgement in high-stakes environments. These are genuinely remarkable capabilities, and organisations that are not leveraging them in their decision-making and governance processes are already operating with a structural disadvantage that will compound as the tools become more widely adopted by their competitors and peers.

What AI is not good at (at this time) is the kind of contextually rich, relationally grounded, failure-tested judgement that comes from decades of working inside complex organisations, navigating the unique human dynamics that never appear in a dataset.

AI can tell you that customer churn is accelerating and that the pattern correlates with a specific service change made eight months ago. It cannot tell you whether the CEO who is defending that service change is genuinely convinced of its merit or is protecting a decision they are no longer confident in and are not yet ready to revisit publicly. AI can surface the fact that management reporting has shifted its emphasis away from the KPIs agreed in the original strategy. It cannot tell you whether that shift reflects a deliberate and considered strategic pivot or a quiet attempt to move the goalposts before anyone notices they have been missed. Those distinctions require the kind of organisational intuition, pattern recognition, and human reading that can only be developed over time, through experience, and through the accumulated exposure to the ways in which organisations and the people inside them actually behave under pressure.

This is where I believe the argument about experienced leadership and AI converges into something genuinely important and, in my view, underappreciated in the current discourse about what AI means for the future of work and leadership.

Just as taking a leadership textbook off the bookshelf and applying it directly as written without appropriate contextualisation to your unique circumstances is likely doomed to failure (or at the minimum, sub-optimal outcomes), I believe the same applies to relying on AI outputs in isolation.

The leaders who will be most formidable in an AI-enabled environment are not necessarily those who adopted the technology earliest or who can navigate the most complex prompting frameworks. They are the ones who bring their battle-scarred years of hard-won and rich experience to the tools, using AI as a super powered partner, to sharpen and validate the judgement they have spent decades building rather than as a substitute for it. The combination of that quality of human experience with the pattern recognition and data processing capability of AI creates a decision-making advantage that neither can replicate independently, and that represents a genuinely new and powerful leadership proposition.

The widening gap between those who engage and those who do not

One of the dynamics I observe consistently as I work across organisations is the progressive widening of a capability gap that is not yet visible in most performance metrics but will be within the next three to five years with near certainty.

On one side of that gap are leaders and organisations who have engaged genuinely and substantively with AI tools. In particular I see those who have moved beyond generic prompts and generic outputs and who have invested the time and the intellectual honesty required to understand where and how these tools add genuine value. They are actively sharing and integrating that capability into how they make decisions, assess performance, and govern their organisations which is great to see. The compounding learning effect of that genuine engagement is significant, because the more fluently you work with these tools and the more context you bring to the interactions, the more substantial and useful the outputs become, which in turn increases the return on the next interaction, and so on.

On the other side are leaders and organisations who are either actively avoiding engagement with AI tools or engaging at the most superficial level: using them occasionally for low-stakes tasks, treating them as a novelty rather than a serious professional instrument, and continuing to make consequential decisions through the same processes they were using three years ago. I want to be direct about this without any judgement attached to the observation, because I was very firmly on that side of the gap twelve months ago and I understand exactly how it happens. The combination of professional confidence (particularly for experienced leaders who have built their careers on the quality of their judgement), unfamiliarity with the technology (perhaps with an element of fear attached), and genuine uncertainty about where AI adds value versus where it introduces risk is a powerful set of forces that make sustained avoidance feel rational in the short term.

What makes it less rational over a longer time horizon is what the tools are now capable of doing in the specific domain that matters most to senior leaders: the quality, rigour, and defensibility of the decisions they make, and the accuracy and independence of the information they use to make them.

Perfection was never the entry requirement. Starting was.

What the governance conversation is missing

I want to spend a moment on the board governance dimension of this argument, because I think it is where the implications of AI adoption are most significant and most consistently under-estimated by the Australian organisations I work with, and by their equivalents in comparable markets globally.

The conversation about AI at board level has, in most organisations I encounter, remained primarily a technology and risk conversation: what are our cyber security exposures, how are we managing data privacy, what is our policy on staff use of AI tools. These are legitimate and important questions. But they are, in a meaningful sense, the wrong primary conversation for a board to be having about AI, because they frame the technology as an operational risk to be managed rather than as a governance instrument that changes the fundamental quality of information available to a board doing its job.

The governance conversation that is most conspicuously absent, and most urgently needed, is around agentic AI: the autonomous systems that are increasingly operating within organisations not simply as analytical tools, but as active decision-making agents.

Where traditional AI tools surface information for human review, agentic AI systems make decisions, execute actions, and manage workflows with minimal or no human involvement at the point of execution. The accountability question this creates for boards is not theoretical; it is immediate. When an agentic system operating on behalf of your organisation makes a consequential error, the current governance architecture of most boards has no clear answer for where accountability sits, how it was authorised, and what the escalation pathway should be. Addressing that gap is one of the most pressing and least discussed governance priorities of the next three years. We will dive deeper into this shortly.

Another question that most boards are not yet systematically asking is: how is AI changing the quality and independence of the information we receive, and are we using the tools available to us to test and triangulate the management narrative we are presented with against the underlying data? The Australian Institute of Company Directors has begun to address this as a governance priority, and the trajectory is clear: within a short number of years, a board that is not actively interrogating the quality of its information environment using the tools now available to it will be viewed as operating with a material governance gap in the same way that a board without adequate financial literacy is viewed today.

For the individual director or executive sitting in that room, the question is both simpler and more urgent: am I bringing the best possible thinking to the decisions I am responsible for, and am I using every tool available to me to ensure that the information those decisions are based on is as accurate, complete, and independently verified as it can be? That question has always been the right one.

Now though, the tools available to answer it have become dramatically more powerful, and more accessible than at any point in the history of modern governance.

When AI stops asking permission: the agentic governance gap

I want to go deeper on a specific dimension of the AI governance conversation that represents territory that most boards are not yet thinking about at all – and the window for getting ahead of it is narrowing faster than most directors appreciate.

The discussion so far has largely centred on AI as an instrument of better governance: a tool that helps boards interrogate management information more independently, surface the early warning signals that human oversight tends to miss, and close the gap between what the data shows and what the prevailing narrative allows people to hear. That framing is accurate and important. But it is also, in an important sense, already becoming incomplete.

The next wave of AI deployment in organisations is not just about better information. It is about autonomous action.

Agentic AI, namely AI systems that do not simply analyse and recommend but take sequential, autonomous actions, make decisions, execute transactions, and operate workflows without requiring human approval at each step, is no longer a theoretical future state. It is already deployed in commercial, legal, financial, and operational contexts in organisations around the world, including, almost certainly, in some of the organisations you are responsible for governing.

And here is the governance problem that keeps me up at night, and that I suspect will occupy boards and regulators for the better part of the next decade: existing governance frameworks were designed for a world in which decisions move through a human chain. Usually we would see that management teams recommend and the board approves or challenges. In the pre-agentic AI world, action follows that formal reflection and approval process.

However, agentic AI collapses that chain entirely. Decisions are made, actions are taken, and consequences are incurred before any board oversight mechanism has a chance to trigger reflection or decisions, sometimes in milliseconds, sometimes across thousands of simultaneous transactions.

If the governance conversation most boards are having about AI is the wrong primary conversation, as I argued earlier in this chapter, then the conversation most boards are not yet having about agentic AI is something more concerning still.

In my work with boards and leadership teams, I have come to think about this as four distinct governance gaps, each of which the existing frameworks: Corporations Act and legislative duties, ASX governance principles, standard risk registers, and current director competency frameworks, all leave substantially unaddressed at present.

1. The accountability vacuum

When an agentic AI system acting on behalf of your organisation makes a decision that causes harm; a discriminatory loan assessment, a safety-compromising operational call, a reputationally damaging communication, then who carries the liability? The director who approved the system's deployment? The CEO who set its operating parameters? The vendor who built it? The legal and regulatory frameworks that govern director duties were not written for a world in which the decision-maker is not a person. That gap is real, it is not yet resolved, and in the meantime the organisations deploying these systems are sitting in it.

2. The oversight paradox

Traditional board oversight rests on a fundamental assumption: that it is possible to review and challenge the decisions management makes. Agentic AI operates at machine speed across volumes of decisions that no board, no audit committee, and no risk function can meaningfully review in human time. You cannot govern what you cannot see, and you cannot see what is moving faster than any human reporting mechanism can capture. The oversight model that has worked for every other governance challenge in the modern era does not work here without significant structural redesign.

3. The risk register gap

Most boards I encounter have categorised AI as a technology risk: a cyber exposure, a data privacy question, an operational process concern. Agentic AI is not a technology risk. It is clearly a decision-making risk, a fiduciary risk, and a reputational risk simultaneously – all at a scale and speed that existing risk taxonomies were not designed to capture. The category is wrong, which means the governance response to it is almost certainly wrong as well.

4. The competency deficit

The AICD's own research is direct on this point: the majority of Australian and international board directors do not yet have the foundational AI literacy to ask the right questions of management about standard AI tools, let alone to govern systems that are making autonomous decisions on behalf of the organisation. The governance gap here is not only structural; it is a competency problem, and it is one that will not be closed by a single board education session or the addition of a "technology director" to the composition conversation.

I raise these not to alarm, and certainly not to suggest that the answer is to slow the deployment of tools that have genuine commercial and organisational value. The answer is almost never to avoid the future. The answer is to be among those who are thinking clearly about it before it arrives, rather than managing the consequences after it does.

What I would put to you and to the board you sit on or advise is this: when did your board last have a conversation specifically about the governance architecture required for agentic AI systems, as distinct from AI tools in general? When did you last ask management to map where autonomous AI decision-making is currently operating in your organisation, at what scale, with what human oversight backstops, and under what liability assumptions?

The AI didn't wait for the board to approve the agenda. It already ran the business.

If the honest answer is that the conversation has not yet happened, that is important information. And the time to have it, as with almost every meaningful governance question I have encountered in my career, is before the decision that makes it urgent.

The human-AI advantage: what it actually looks like in practice

The combination of "experienced leadership" and "AI capability" can sound like an abstract proposition when stated at the level of principle. In practice, the advantage I am describing shows up in specific and observable ways that are increasingly distinguishable from the outputs of either human judgement or AI analysis alone.

When I work through a complex organisational challenge with an advisory client now, the process looks materially different from what it looked like two years ago.

The analytical foundation of a strategic assessment, is specifically:

- the research into comparable situations,
- the stress-testing of assumptions,
- the mapping of second and third-order consequences, and
- the drafting of scenarios for how different decisions are likely to play out given the specific characteristics of the organisation and the market it operates in.

All of those elements above can now be done faster, more thoroughly, and with a greater degree of analytical rigour with AI than was possible when the process depended entirely on human time and human processing capacity.

What it cannot do and what remains irreplaceable in that process is *the interpretation of what the analysis means in the specific human and organisational context of that client*: the reading of the dynamics in the room, the understanding of what the CEO is not saying as much as what they are, the knowledge of which recommendations will and *realistically can* be genuinely implemented and which will be politely received and quietly shelved, the judgement about where the real leverage point in the system actually lies. Those elements are the product of years of accumulated experience by individuals that no model can replicate, and they are what determine whether a genuinely excellent piece of analysis translates into a genuinely useful outcome for the organisation.

The combination of those two things: the analytical depth and speed of AI with the contextual, relational, and experiential richness of sustained leadership practice, is what I have come to believe represents the most significant and durable competitive advantage available to experienced leaders in the current environment.

Not AI alone, which without contextual judgement is at best very sophisticated pattern-matching and at worst overly confident and articulate hallucination (that's AI speak for B#llsh$t!). Not human experience alone, which without the analytical leverage of AI is increasingly slow, expensive, and subject to cognitive biases and relational distortion. But the deliberate, thoughtful, continuously refined integration of both, which produces outcomes that are genuinely better than either could achieve independently.

For now, the point I want to leave you with is simpler and more immediately actionable.

The permission to begin where you are

One of the things I most wish someone had said to me twelve months ago, when I was sitting on the wrong side of the AI gap and feeling anxious and uncertain about where to start, is that the sophistication of where you begin matters far less than the decision to just start with genuine curious intent.

The experience that makes senior leaders valuable: the pattern recognition, the organisational intuition, the failure-tested judgement that cannot be acquired any other way, does not diminish in an AI-enabled environment. It becomes more valuable, not less, because it provides the contextual richness that transforms good AI output into genuinely exceptional insight. What changes is that this experience, applied alongside the right tools and with a genuine commitment to understanding where and how they add value, compounds in ways that create an entirely new quality of professional capability.

The leaders I see making the greatest gains in our current AI operating environment are not those who started earliest or who have the deepest technical knowledge of how the models work. They are the ones who are most honest about the gap between what they currently know and what they need to know, most committed to closing that gap through genuine engagement rather than performative familiarity, and most willing to be honest in distinguishing between the cases where AI is genuinely improving their thinking and those where it is simply confirming what they already believed, just in more impressive language.

That last point is worth sitting with for a moment. One of the subtler risks of AI adoption for leaders is not scepticism but the opposite. There is a natural human tendency to use these tools in ways that reinforce existing beliefs rather than genuinely challenge them, and to treat the fluency and authority of a well-constructed AI output as evidence of its correctness rather than as a reason to interrogate and contextualise it with the same discipline you would apply to any other source.

The tools that are most valuable are the ones that make your thinking better, not the ones that make it sound better and that distinction is important. Learning to distinguish between those two outcomes is, in my experience, one of the most important and most underappreciated skills in the entire landscape of effective AI adoption.

What AI sees and what that means for how you lead

I want to close this chapter by returning to its title, because the most important thing AI sees in organisations is not the metric drift, the reporting inconsistencies, or the early signals of performance deterioration, though it sees these with greater consistency and less relational bias than any human observer. The most important thing AI sees is the gap between intention and reality, at a level of specificity and independence that makes the gap much harder to paper over or explain away.

For organisations that have been operating with genuine discipline and transparency, that clarity is an enormous asset because it provides the kind of early, actionable intelligence that allows problems to be addressed when they are still small. For organisations that have been managing primarily through narrative, relationship, and the natural human reluctance to challenge those in positions of authority and trust, it represents a fundamentally changed operating environment.

The leaders who will thrive in that environment are not those who find the most sophisticated ways to manage their AI tools' outputs, but those who use the clarity those tools provide to do what good leadership has always required: seeing what is actually happening in their organisations with accuracy, full transparency and honesty, making decisions based on evidence rather than narrative, holding themselves and others to standards that are genuinely applied rather than selectively enforced, and bringing the depth of human experience and judgement to bear on the questions that data alone cannot answer.

That combination is what I mean when I talk about the ***experience-intelligence edge*** and it is what makes experienced leaders genuinely and increasingly formidable.

We will return to this argument in Chapter 11. In the chapters between here and there, we move into the practical playbooks where the principles explored earlier translate into specific, actionable frameworks for leaders who are ready to put them to work.

AI does not create the Discipline Dividend. It makes it more measurable, more visible, and, in organisations that have already built the disciplined architecture, significantly more powerful. For organisations that have not, it simply makes the cost of the absent dividend harder to ignore.

TOOLBOX — Chapter 7

Questions to examine your own AI adoption and the governance implications for your organisation
Use these questions to honestly assess where you and your organisation currently sit in relation to AI adoption, and to identify the most meaningful next steps in building the human-AI advantage described in this chapter.

A. Questions to honestly assess your own AI engagement
1. Where on the spectrum from generic requests to genuine professional integration does my current AI engagement sit, and am I being honest with myself about that?
2. When I use AI tools in my professional work, am I genuinely inviting challenge and counter-argument, or am I primarily seeking validation for positions I have already formed?
3. What is the quality difference between the outputs I receive now compared with six months ago, and what does that trajectory tell me about the depth of my engagement?
4. Which aspects of my professional work would benefit most from the kind of analytical depth, speed, and pattern recognition that AI tools provide, and am I actively applying them there?
5. What is the honest reason I have not yet engaged with AI tools more deeply, and is that reason likely to become more or less defensible over the next twelve months?

B. Questions about where experience adds most value
1. In the most consequential decisions I have made in the past twelve months, what would have been different if I had had

access to more rigorous, independently derived analytical support?

2. Where in my professional work is the gap between "what the data says" and "what I know from experience about how this situation actually works" most significant, and how am I navigating that gap currently?

3. Which of the patterns I see in my work most clearly reflect the kind of contextual, relational, failure-tested judgement that AI cannot replicate, and am I applying that judgement as deliberately and explicitly as I could be?

4. Where is my experience currently most under-utilised, and would better analytical tools change that?

5. What would it look like to bring my full depth of experience to bear on the most important problem I am currently working on, with the best available AI analytical support alongside it?

C. Questions for boards and executive Teams on the governance dimension

1. Is our board conversation about AI primarily a risk and technology conversation, or have we begun to treat it as a governance capability question that affects the quality of the information and decisions we are responsible for?

2. How confident are we that the management information we receive is being independently tested and validated, rather than being accepted primarily on the basis of our trust in the leadership team presenting it?

3. Are there AI-enabled analytics tools available to us that would materially improve the independence and rigour of our governance oversight, and if so, what is preventing us from using them?

4. Where in our current governance processes is the gap between "what the data shows" and "what we are being told the data shows" most likely to exist, and how would we know if it did?

5. In three years, looking back at this period of AI adoption, what would we most regret not having done earlier at a governance and decision-making level?

D. Questions about distinguishing genuine improvement from impressive output

1. How do I currently distinguish between an AI output that has genuinely improved my thinking and one that has simply articulated my existing position more fluently and authoritatively?
2. Where in my AI usage am I most at risk of confirmation bias: prompting in ways that generate validation rather than genuine challenge?
3. What would it look like to deliberately use AI as an adversarial thinking partner rather than a supportive one, and where in my current work would that be most valuable?
4. How am I building the habit of interrogating AI outputs with the same critical discipline I would apply to any other source of information or advice?
5. Where has AI already changed my thinking in a way I did not anticipate, and what does that tell me about where the greatest remaining value might lie?

E. Questions about building the human-AI advantage over time

1. What is my specific, committed plan to close the gap between where my AI capability currently sits and where I genuinely need it to be, and have I allocated the time and resources to make that plan realistic?
2. Who in my professional network is furthest ahead in their genuine integration of AI into their leadership and advisory practice, and am I actively learning from them?
3. Where is the combination of my specific depth of experience with AI analytical capability most likely to produce

a genuinely differentiated professional outcome, and am I pursuing that combination deliberately?

4. How will I know, twelve months from now, whether my AI engagement has genuinely improved the quality of my decisions and the value I deliver, and am I measuring the right things to make that assessment?

5. What is the single most important next step I could take this week to begin genuinely building the experience-intelligence edge described in this chapter?

F. Questions for boards on governing agentic AI

Use these questions to assess your board's current readiness to govern agentic AI systems: those that take autonomous actions and make decisions without human approval or oversight at each step.

On awareness and deployment

1. Does our board have a clear, current picture of where agentic AI is already operating within our organisation; across which functions, at what scale, and with what decision-making authority, or are we relying on management to tell us when it becomes relevant?

2. Have we asked management to specifically distinguish between AI tools that assist human decisions and AI systems that make or execute decisions autonomously? Do we understand the difference in governance terms?

3. When did we last receive a board-level briefing that specifically addressed agentic AI deployment, as distinct from AI policy and technology risk more broadly?

On accountability

1. If an agentic AI system operating within our organisation made a decision today that caused material harm to a cus-

tomer, employee, or third party, could we clearly articulate
where the accountability sits and would that answer hold up
under legal scrutiny?
2. Have we sought advice on how our existing director duty
obligations apply to decisions made by autonomous AI systems acting on behalf of the organisation? If not, what is
preventing us from doing so?
3. Are there agentic AI systems currently operating in our
organisation whose parameters were set by management
without explicit board-level visibility or approval? Should
there be a threshold above which board sign-off is required?

On oversight

1. What oversight mechanisms currently exist for decisions
made by agentic AI systems in our organisation, and are
those mechanisms operating at a speed and scale that is
actually commensurate with the volume and velocity of the
decisions being made?
2. Is there a human override or escalation protocol embedded in every agentic AI system we operate, and when did
the board last verify that those protocols are functioning as
designed?
3. How would we know, at a board level, if an agentic AI system in our organisation began operating outside its intended
parameters? What is the detection and escalation pathway?

On risk

1. Does our current risk register accurately reflect agentic AI as a
decision-making risk, a fiduciary risk, and a reputational risk
or is it currently categorised primarily as a technology or operational risk? What would need to change to correct that?

1. Have we stress-tested our organisation's risk appetite statement against a scenario in which an agentic AI system makes a consequential error at scale? Does our current framework provide adequate guidance for that scenario?
2. Which of our existing risk management frameworks: cyber, legal, operational, reputational, would be triggered first if an agentic AI deployment caused harm, and are we comfortable that the response those frameworks prescribe would be adequate?

On competency

1. Honestly assessed, does our board have sufficient collective AI literacy to ask genuinely probing questions of management about agentic AI deployment or are we largely reliant on management and vendors to frame what we should be asking?
2. What is our board's specific plan to build the foundational AI competency required to govern agentic systems effectively, and does that plan have a timeline and an owner?
3. Who on our board or in our advisory network has the depth of knowledge required to help us distinguish between management's assessment of agentic AI risk and an independently formed view? If no-one, how do we address that gap?

Looking forward

1. In three years, if agentic AI has caused a material governance failure in an organisation comparable to ours, what would we most regret not having asked or addressed during this period?
2. Are we governing agentic AI with the same rigour and discipline we would apply to a major capital allocation or a significant acquisition and if not, does the risk profile warrant that we should be?

Closing Reflection — Chapter 7

The tools that are now available to us do not diminish what experience has built. They amplify it but only if we bring the intellectual honesty and genuine engagement required to use them well.

The gap between those who do and those who do not is widening, quietly and without drama, in the same way that all of the most consequential gaps in organisations do. The time to engage with that reality is not when the gap has become impossible to close, but now, while the compound returns on genuine engagement are still available to be earned.

What you bring to these tools matters more than the tools themselves. But only if you actually bring it.

Here is a space for your own reflection on this chapter. What resonated with you

(Write your thoughts here)

THE ACCOUNTABILITY PLAYBOOK: REBUILDING THE LINE AFTER IT HAS BEEN LOST

"The time to repair the roof is when the sun is shining."
—John F. Kennedy,
35th President of the United States

You don't rebuild accountability with a memo.
You rebuild it one play at a time.

Up to this point, this book has focused primarily on making the problem visible: how drift, avoidance, blurred standards, and unsupported accountability take hold in organisations and quietly become normal. From here, the focus shifts more explicitly to practical and pragmatic solutions (which is the whole point of the book).

The chapters that follow are practical playbooks designed to help leaders rebuild the lines in accountability, in judgement, in capability, and in culture, using disciplined structures that can be successfully applied in the real world, not just admired in theory.

There is a moment I have never forgotten, and one that I suspect will resonate with anyone who has ever walked into an organisation mid-transformation and discovered that the cultural problems they were dealing with were significantly deeper and more systemic than the operational ones they had been sent to fix.

I was several months into the North American integration, working across the three previously independent geographic regions that we were consolidating into a single operating entity. As I described in Chapter 2, each of those regions had been allowed enormous autonomy for years, and each had developed its own distinct leadership culture, its own operating rhythms, and its own unspoken set of norms around what constituted acceptable performance. Part of my task was to bring those three very different cultures into meaningful alignment, which in practice meant understanding precisely how far apart they were before I could begin to close the gap.

I thought I had a reasonable read on that gap. Oh boy, was I wrong.

One evening I attended a monthly event in one of the country operations that we called a "Buzz Night," which in concept is exactly what good recognition and motivation events should be. It was a celebration of individual and team wins from the past month, a moment to reinforce the behaviours and results that matter, and a reset of focus and energy heading into the month ahead. When they are run well, these events are genuinely powerful culture drivers, and I was looking forward to seeing how this particular region ran theirs.

The previous month's financial results had only just been finalised, and I had been quietly briefed by the CFO in the minutes immediately before the proceedings started, that they were truly terrible. We had made a significant loss again in that region, continuing a trend that was exactly the kind of result the entire transformation had been mobilised to address.

What happened next genuinely stunned me.

The country leader stepped up on stage, took a breath, and proudly announced to the entire assembled team that they had made profit for the previous month. The room erupted in cheering and applause.

I stood very still and said nothing, though every instinct I had was screaming. Had I somehow misheard the numbers the CFO had given me minutes earlier? Unfortunately, when I confirmed the results with the CFO immediately after the event, I had not misheard a single figure. The leader had simply chosen to not let the truth get in the way of a good celebration!

When I questioned the leader directly and privately afterward, asking why they had made the decision to misstate the result, the response I received was delivered with complete sincerity and what I understood to be genuine intent. They explained that hearing about losses was not motivating, and that the belief that they were making profit would be more inspiring for the team.

This person was not being malicious. I believe they were, in their own framework, trying to lead well. And that is precisely what made that moment instructive and alarming to me in equal measure, because what had not been recognised (and what became crystal clear to me in that moment) was that in taking that approach, accountability had not just been softened or deferred. It had been dissolved.

The leader had let them think that they were already doing what was necessary for the business to turn around. This was far from the truth.

What was clear to me was that the perceived level of effort and performance required to be profitable was totally out of alignment with the actual commercial reality of the business. This outcome was not a single bad decision on that night. It was the visible expression of a cultural norm that had been building quietly for years, in which protecting morale had been permitted, gradually and without deliberate intent, to create a comfortable bubble for the team where feelings were more important than facts.

Things changed immediately from that night forward, and I embarked on what became one of the most deliberate and demanding cultural resets I have ever had to engineer: total and radical transparency across results, expectations, performance outcomes, and standards, alongside a complete recalibration of what genuine recognition, celebration, and reward looked like in that context. It was neither quick nor easy, because unwinding the behaviours and cultural assumptions that had led us to that Buzz Night took considerable time and effort, and some deeply uncomfortable conversations with people who believed they were doing the right thing in fostering the 'unicorns and rainbows' approach to the unpleasant financial details the team really needed to know.

But it taught me something about the architecture of accountability resets that I have applied in every significant intervention since, and that forms the foundation of this chapter.

Why accountability resets fail before they begin

The most common mistake I observe when organisations attempt to rebuild accountability after it has broken down at scale is that they begin with the intervention before they have completed the diagnosis. They identify the visible symptom – in this case a leader who is not holding their team to standards, a set of results that has been persistently explained rather than interrogated, a culture in which difficult conversations are chronically deferred – and they respond to that symptom directly, through a new performance framework, a leadership communication, a values refresh, or a governance restructure.

These interventions are not always wrong, but they are almost always premature, because the symptom they are responding to is rarely the root cause of the breakdown. The leader who misrepresented the financial results to his team was a symptom. The root cause was a cultural operating norm, embedded across years of autonomous and empowered leadership without aligned standards, that had made comfortable fiction more socially and professionally acceptable than uncomfortable truth. Immediately addressing the individual leader directly, which I did, was nowhere near sufficient to deal with the issue. Without simultaneously addressing the systemic cultural norm that had made that behaviour feel not just acceptable but arguably responsible, the same pattern would simply have re-emerged under different management.

This is the fundamental reason why accountability resets are harder than accountability maintenance, and why the playbook for rebuilding accountability from a degraded base is meaningfully different from the playbook for holding it in an organisation where it has never fully collapsed.

Diagnosing before you intervene: the Root Cause Framework©

The diagnostic tool I have used most consistently as the foundation for accountability resets is a framework I have developed and refined across thirty years of working inside and alongside organisations of significantly different sizes, sectors, and levels of cultural complexity. I call it the Root Cause Diagnostic Framework©, and its central premise is straightforward: before you can address an accountability problem that has embedded itself systemically, you need to understand precisely which of the six root cause domains is driving it, because the intervention required differs substantially depending on where the true cause lives.

It is no different to the approach a capable physician uses when addressing the physical symptoms their patients arrive with; thoroughly exploring the potential root cause issues to ascertain the true causality of the symptom or issue before being able to address it effectively. Too often in my corporate experience, the root cause is not identified by the presenting organisational "symptoms". Many organisations exclusively focus on addressing what is right in front of them (fighting fires) and not simultaneously digging in to ascertain the root cause so that it can be properly addressed.

The six domains of this framework are as follows.

The first is **structural accountability**, which addresses the question of whether ownership and responsibility are genuinely clear at every level of the organisation. Not just on paper, but in practice, in how decisions are made, how performance is reported, and how consequences are applied when expectations are not met. The most common structural accountability failure I encounter is shared accountability constructs that, as I described in Chapter 4, effectively mean accountability belongs explicitly to no-one at the point where it matters most.

The second is **cultural norms and accepted behaviours**, which addresses the question of what the organisation actually tolerates and rewards in practice, as distinct from what it says it values in its stated frameworks and communications. The Buzz Night story is a near-perfect illustration of a cultural norm failure: the stated organisational value was transparency and performance, but the actual unspoken cultural norm was that protecting motivation justified misrepresenting reality.

The third is **leadership capability and style**, which addresses the question of whether the leaders responsible for holding accountability genuinely have the skills, the emotional capability, and the professional confidence to have the direct and sometimes uncomfortable conversations that real accountability requires. This domain is often the one most organisations reach for first, because investing in leadership development feels constructive and forward-facing. But it is frequently not the root cause, and in organisations where the structural and cultural foundations are broken, improved leadership capability without concurrent structural and cultural repair simply produces more articulate avoidance of the same underlying problems.

The fourth is **systems and process alignment**, which addresses the question of whether the measurement, reporting, and governance systems of the organisation are designed in a way that supports accountability rather than inadvertently undermining it. Organisations where the metrics reported to leadership and the board have gradually migrated away from the indicators that would most clearly signal a problem (which is the metric drift pattern I described in Chapter 6) are experiencing a systems and process alignment failure.

The fifth is **individual capability gaps**, which addresses the question of whether the people in specific roles genuinely have the capability, knowledge, and competence, to meet the expectations they are being held to. This domain is the one most frequently misdiagnosed as a motivation or attitude problem, and its misidentification has significant consequences. Holding people accountable to standards they do not yet have the capability to meet produces anxiety, gaming, and ultimately attrition of exactly the people the organisation most needs to develop.

The sixth is **external environmental factors**, which addresses the question of whether there are genuine market, competitive, or contextual factors materially contributing to the performance gap, and whether the organisation's current accountability architecture adequately distinguishes between what is within the control of its people and what is not. This domain is the *one most commonly misused*, in both directions: either ignored entirely in punitive accountability cultures that hold people responsible for outcomes shaped by factors outside anyone's control, or over-relied upon in avoidance cultures where almost any performance gap can be contextualised with sufficient narrative creativity.

The diagnostic power of this framework lies not in its individual domains, but in the discipline of working through all six before reaching a conclusion about where the primary root cause of an accountability breakdown actually resides. In recognising these, as is almost always the case in genuine cultural resets, the answer is rarely confined to a single domain.

In the North American situation I described, an honest diagnostic would have identified: primary root causes in cultural norms and accepted behaviours (the Buzz Night story); structural accountability (three regions operating with entirely different performance standards and no unified baseline); and systems and process alignment (the absence of consolidated, reliable reporting that I described in Chapter 4 as one of the defining features of that first planning meeting). Leadership capability was a contributing factor in specific cases but not the primary driver. Individual capability gaps existed but were largely secondary to the structural and cultural environment those individuals were operating in. External environmental factors were genuinely significant; 9/11 had fundamentally disrupted the core business and operating model but were being used in some parts of the organisation as cover for performance issues that pre-dated the disruption.

That diagnosis dictated a reset sequence that addressed the structural and cultural domains first, because until those foundations were rebuilt, improved leadership conversations and better individual capability development would have had nowhere solid to land.

The sequence matters as much as the intervention

One of the judgements that leaders find most difficult is not what to fix but in what order to fix it. This is particularly true when, commonly, multiple domains require simultaneous attention, and there is neither the time nor the organisational bandwidth to address everything at once with equal intensity.

In my experience, the sequencing that produces the most durable results consistently begins with what I think of as the visibility and clarity foundations, before moving to the structural and then the behavioural work. Finally, the approach moves to the reinforcement and recognition architecture. This determines whether the reset holds over time or slowly reverts to the previous operating norm under the pressure of competing priorities and the natural human preference for comfort over accountability.

The visibility and clarity foundation is the work of establishing, as clearly and as transparently as possible, what the actual current state of performance is, measured against standards. In the North American context, this was the work of radical transparency: establishing what the real financial results were, what the genuine performance gap looked like, and what the actual minimum acceptable standards were across all three regions, in a way that left no room for the kind of creative reinterpretation that had produced the Buzz Night announcement.

This is frequently the most uncomfortable step in a reset, because it requires the organisation to look honestly at the gap between what it has been telling itself and what the evidence actually shows, and that discomfort is real and should not be minimised. But it is non-negotiable, because a reset built on a softened assessment of the starting point will simply replicate, at a slightly higher level, the same pattern of comfortable ambiguity that allowed the breakdown to embed in the first place.

The structural work that follows is that of ensuring that ownership, decision rights, reporting accountability, and escalation pathways are clear, unambiguous, and genuinely embedded. This is where the discipline of asking (in the way I described in Chapter 4) "who is ultimately responsible for this outcome, not as a team, not as a working group, but as a single named individual," produces its most significant value.

Shared accountability constructs that have drifted into genuine diffusion of ownership, need to be explicitly unwound and replaced with clear, singular accountability at every consequential level of the organisation. This must be supported by the governance and reporting mechanisms that make that ownership visible and impossible to quietly reassign when things become difficult.

The behavioural re-framing is the work of addressing, directly and specifically, the cultural norms that allowed the accountability breakdown to develop and persist. This is where the individual accountability conversation skills described in Chapter 5 are deployed at scale, across every leadership level simultaneously, rather than in isolated cases.

The reason this work must follow rather than precede the structural work is that *behavioural change in organisations is enormously difficult to sustain when the structural environment continues to reward the old behaviours.* Leaders who genuinely want to hold their teams to clearer standards will find it much harder to do so if the reporting systems still allow metric drift, if ownership is still diffuse enough to make consequences feel unfair, and if the cultural norm of "glossing over results" is still being modelled by the most senior leaders in the room.

The reinforcement and recognition architecture is the work that determines whether the reset holds over a twelve to twenty-four month horizon, which is the minimum timeframe required for a genuine cultural reset to become self-sustaining rather than dependent on the continued presence and energy of the person who drove it.

Recognition systems that were previously rewarding narrative and relationship management at the expense of genuine performance outcomes need to be explicitly recalibrated, in the same way that the recognition and reward elements of the North American Buzz Nights needed to be rebuilt around honest results rather than imaginary ones. This is not a minor adjustment. From my experience it is often the most politically sensitive part of a reset, because it involves explicitly changing what the organisation celebrates, and some of the people who have been most celebrated under the old system will be among those who find the transition most confronting.

When the senior team is part of the problem

I want to address directly a dynamic that is present in almost every significant accountability reset I have been involved in, and that is rarely discussed honestly because it is deeply uncomfortable: the situation where some of the people who should be the most visible and credible advocates for the accountability reset are among those whose own behaviour and standards need to change for the reset to be genuine. This extends right up to the C-Suite and CEO level.

The most expensive room in the building is a senior team that has stopped telling the truth.

This dynamic is not unusual. It is, in fact, almost structurally inevitable in organisations where accountability has drifted at a systemic level, because that drift does not occur in isolation at the frontline or in middle management while senior leadership maintains its standards intact. Drift is typically modelled from the top down, which means that by the time a genuine accountability reset is required, the senior leadership team itself has usually initiated and embedded some version of the same patterns it is now being asked to correct in others.

The leadership challenge this creates is one of the most delicate I know: how do you drive an accountability reset that requires visible senior modelling and genuine cultural change at the top, without either publicly undermining the credibility of the leaders you need to partner with to deliver it, or allowing those leaders to position themselves as advocates for a change they are not genuinely willing to make in their own behaviour?

In my experience, the answer lies in having the most difficult conversations first and in private, before the reset is publicly announced or communicated broadly. Every member of the senior leadership team needs to understand, what the reset requires of them personally, what the gaps are between their current behaviour and the standard the reset is being built on, and what the consequences are if those gaps are not closed within the reset timeframe.

These are not comfortable conversations, and in some cases they will result in a conclusion that a specific individual cannot make the transition required and that their departure needs to be part of the reset architecture rather than an outcome of its failure. That is a harder early decision than most organisations want to make, but it is nearly always preferable to the alternative: launching a public cultural reset with a senior team that is privately uncommitted to it, and discovering six months later that the visible enthusiasm of the launch has dissolved into the same patterns the reset was designed to address.

Rebuilding trust in a system that has been gamed

Research on procedural fairness consistently shows that people are more willing to accept tough feedback and even negative outcomes when the process is clear, consistent, and transparently linked to agreed standards.

In organisations where accountability has drifted, people's problem is rarely with high standards. Their problem is with selective enforcement and opaque decision-making. Rebuilding trust means demonstrating, repeatedly, that the standard now applies in the same way to everyone.

One of the most challenging issues is that the people inside the organisation have often, entirely rationally, stopped believing that the system is real. They have seen standards stated and then quietly abandoned in the reality of day-to-day leadership practices. They have watched consequences promised and then not delivered. They have participated in performance cycles that felt like "tick the box" theatre rather than genuine management and performance enhancement, and they have adjusted their own behaviour accordingly.

I see this played out by people investing less in meeting the stated standards and more in managing the narrative around them, because that is what their experience has shown them actually matters and carries more weight.

Rebuilding genuine belief in a performance system that has been gamed requires something that cannot be faked and cannot be rushed: the sustained, consistent, and visible application of the new standards over a long enough period that people begin to update their mental model of what the organisation actually does, as distinct from what it says.

I have found that the single most powerful signal in an accountability reset is not the communication of new standards: it is the first time a consequence is clearly and fairly applied to someone who would previously have been protected from it. This is often referred to as the "sacrificial lamb," where the implications of an individual's failure (regardless of tenure) to meet required standards is more publicly (and appropriately) broadcast across the business to ensure everyone understands the consequences of continued non-adherence to standards or acceptable agreed performance standards or behaviours.

That moment, handled well, does more to rebuild organisational belief in the reality of the reset than any number of leadership communications, values workshops, or framework updates, because it demonstrates through action rather than language that this time something is genuinely different.

The corollary is equally important: the first time the new standards are visibly not applied; the first exception; the first protected individual; the first quietly adjusted expectation. At this point we usually see the reset begins to unravel, and the unravelling often happens faster than the building because the organisation's scepticism about whether standards are real is already primed and waiting for evidence to confirm itself.

This is why consistency in the early stages of an accountability reset is more important than perfection, and why the sequencing I described earlier, specifically: visibility first, then structure, then behaviour, then reinforcement, is not a recommendation but a requirement.

Each stage creates the conditions under which the next can succeed, and the loss of integrity at any point in the sequence compromises not just that stage but the credibility of everything that follows.

What radical transparency actually looks like in practice

I want to be specific about what I mean by the phrase "radical transparency", because it is frequently misunderstood as a communication principle when it is actually a governance and leadership discipline.

Radical transparency in the context of an accountability reset does not mean sharing every piece of information with everyone in the organisation regardless of context or consequence. It means ensuring that the people responsible for delivering specific outcomes have access to accurate, complete, and timely information in order to act effectively.

Importantly it also implies that they receive that information in a way that treats them as capable adults rather than as fragile recipients who need to be protected from the reality of their own performance.

In the North American context, this translated into a complete overhaul of how results were communicated at every level of the organisation, from the executive team through to the individual region and country operations. We replaced the various customised and selectively positive versions of performance communication with a single, consistent, honest account of where we stood, what the gap was, what we needed to do to close it, and what progress against that target looked like month by month.

The initial discomfort of that shift was real and significant, particularly in regions where the gap between the communicated performance story and the actual results was largest.

But the productive consequence of that discomfort was a level of collective understanding of the actual challenge we faced that had not previously existed.

That understanding, uncomfortable as it was, combined with a unified "call to action" and a clear and compelling picture of the "Brightness of Future" for us when we achieved the desired outcomes, was the foundation on which genuine commitment to the transformation could be built.

People cannot commit to closing a gap they do not know exists. They cannot take ownership of a performance problem they have been told does not exist. And they cannot build confidence in their capability to improve results if the feedback they receive tells them what their leader thinks they need to hear rather than what they actually need to know.

The role of AI in accountability resets

As I noted at the close of Chapter 7, AI is progressively removing the places where accountability failures can hide, and that dynamic is particularly relevant to the accountability reset architecture I have described in this Chapter.

The diagnostic work that underlies an effective reset, namely the honest identification of where performance has actually been and how far it has drifted from the stated standard, has historically been one of the most politically complex parts of the process.

Mainly because it requires surfacing information that people with an interest in the existing narrative have often had the ability to obscure, contextualise, or simply not produce.

AI-enabled analytics, applied to the data organisations already collect, can accelerate and depoliticise that diagnostic work significantly. It provides an independent and consistent analysis of performance trends, metric drift, and governance anomalies that does not require the political courage of a human challenger to surface. This usually provides impartial analysis that is considerably harder to dismiss as a matter of interpretation or perspective.

For organisations in the early stages of an accountability reset, this is a genuinely powerful capability, and one that I would encourage any leader to explore seriously before relying exclusively on the management information that has been produced by the system they are trying to change. The independence of the analytical lens matters as much as the quality of the data it is applied to, and AI-enabled analysis applied to raw underlying data rather than curated management reporting can frequently surface the gap between what the organisation has been told and what has actually been happening.

What AI cannot do, is have the direct, honest, and human conversation that is required to move from contextual diagnosis to action. Nor can it make the leadership judgement about which root cause to address first, which individuals are willing to change and which need to leave, and how to rebuild genuine organisational belief in the reality of a new standard over time. Those are the enduring human dimensions of accountability leadership, and they require exactly the combination of experience, contextual judgment, and disciplined empathy that this book has been exploring from its first chapter.

The psychosocial governance obligation: what boards must now own

There is one further dimension of the accountability reset architecture that boards and executive leadership teams need to understand with far greater clarity than most currently do, and it connects the argument of this entire chapter directly to the legal landscape I described in Chapter 5.

As of late 2025, Australia's nationally consistent psychosocial hazard regulations place psychological health on exactly the same legal footing as physical safety risks. The obligations they create for boards are not advisory: they are mandatory and they are enforceable. The same framework creates comparable obligations across the United Kingdom, Canada, and most comparable international jurisdictions.

In December 2025, the Australian Department of Defence was convicted in the NSW Local Court, becoming the first Commonwealth employer in Australia's history to be found guilty of failing to manage psychosocial risks under federal work health and safety law.

The case arose from a performance management process that the department's own supervisors were inadequately trained to administer safely. The worker, an RAAF technician displaying increasing signs of distress throughout, received no referral for support, no leave, and no relief from the process that was generating the risk. Defence pleaded guilty under the Commonwealth Work Health and Safety Act 2011 and was fined $188,000, with an adverse publicity order imposed alongside it. It was the first such conviction. It will not be the last, and the pattern of enforcement is moving decisively in one direction.

What most boards have not yet fully internalised is that the psychosocial risk framework does not simply create liability for individual leadership behaviours. It creates liability for the *governance architecture* that allows those behaviours to persist undetected or unaddressed. Chronic ambiguity about performance expectations, the systematic avoidance of accountability conversations, the tolerance of a high-performing individual whose behaviour creates fear and uncertainty in the people around them; each of these is now a documentable psychosocial hazard for which the board carries governance responsibility, not just the operational leader closest to it.

This means that the accountability reset architecture described in this chapter is no longer purely a leadership and culture matter. It is a board governance matter, and boards that are not actively monitoring the psychosocial risk profile of their organisations with the same rigour they would apply to financial, operational, and reputational risk, are operating with an increasingly visible governance gap. The metrics that belong in board reporting are not complicated: role clarity scores from engagement surveys; patterns in grievance and complaint data; turnover rates in specific teams or functions. The consistency with which performance standards are applied across comparable situations are all signals that a well-governed board should be asking to see and to understand over time.

The organisations that will navigate this landscape best are those whose boards treat the accountability reset not as a management intervention to be observed from a distance, but as a governance priority to be owned at the highest level, because that is precisely what the legislation now requires, and what the evidence of organisational performance, over time, consistently supports.

TOOLBOX — Chapter 8

Questions to diagnose, sequence, and sustain an accountability reset

These questions are designed to help you apply the Root Cause Diagnostic Framework© and the accountability reset architecture described in this chapter to your own organisation, team, or advisory context. Work through them slowly and honestly, and resist the instinct to reach for an intervention before the diagnosis is complete.

A. Questions to diagnose the root cause domain

1. Where in this organisation has accountability genuinely broken down, and how long has that breakdown been developing beneath the surface before it became visible?

2. Which of the six root cause domains; structural accountability, cultural norms, leadership capability, systems and process alignment, individual capability gaps, or external environmental factors is most clearly driving the pattern I am observing?

3. Am I confident that what I am treating as the root cause is not itself a symptom of something deeper and less visible?

4. Where in this organisation is the gap between what is stated as the performance standard and what is actually tolerated in practice most significant?

5. What would an honest diagnostic of our performance communication tell us about the difference between what people have been told and what has actually been happening?

B. Questions to test whether the senior team Is part of the reset

1. Which members of the senior leadership team most need to change their own behaviour for this reset to be credible, and have I had direct, private, and specific conversations with each of them about what that change requires?

2. Where is the enthusiasm for the accountability reset among the senior team genuine, where is it performative and what is the difference between those two groups telling me?

3. What would happen to the reset if I removed my own direct presence and energy from the equation, and what does that tell me about how deeply the commitment has actually embedded at the senior level?

4. Which individuals in the senior team cannot or will not make the transition this reset requires, and have I been honest with myself about what that means for the architecture of the reset?

5. What am I modelling in my own behaviour that is consistent with the accountability standards I am asking others to meet, and where are there gaps I have not yet addressed?

C. Questions about the sequencing of the reset

1. Have I completed the visibility and clarity foundation work before moving to structural and behavioural interventions, and am I confident that the organisation has a shared and honest understanding of the actual current state?

2. Which domain requires the most urgent attention, and am I addressing it in an order that creates the conditions for subsequent interventions to succeed rather than simply stacking them simultaneously?

3. What is the first visible consequence that will demonstrate to the organisation that this reset is real rather than

another round of management theatre, and am I prepared to deliver it?

4. Where have I allowed the discomfort of the reset to cause me to slow the sequence or soften the standard, and what has that cost in terms of organisational belief?

5. What is my twelve-month horizon plan for the reinforcement and recognition architecture, and have I explicitly recalibrated what the organisation celebrates to reflect the new standard rather than the old one?

D. Questions about rebuilding belief in the system

1. Do the people in this organisation genuinely believe that the performance standards being set will be consistently applied, or do they believe this is another version of a pattern they have seen before?

2. What evidence from our own recent history would a sceptical employee point to in order to justify their disbelief in the reality of this reset, and have I addressed those specific incidents directly?

3. How long has it been since a consequence was clearly and fairly applied to someone who would previously have been protected from it, and what message has that timeline sent to the organisation?

4. Where in our current performance and recognition systems are we still inadvertently rewarding narrative management rather than genuine performance, and what specific change is required to address that?

5. What would need to be consistently true for twelve months for a genuinely sceptical long-term employee to conclude that something has fundamentally changed in how this organisation operates?

E. Questions about radical transparency

1. Are the people responsible for delivering specific outcomes receiving accurate, complete, and timely information about their own performance against the agreed standard, or are they receiving a version of that information that has been filtered for motivational effect?

2. Where in our performance communication architecture is selective positivity creating the same dynamic that produced the Buzz Night story; people operating against a performance reality they have not been accurately told?

3. What information is the senior leadership team receiving about organisational performance that is not making its way to the people responsible for improving it, and what is the justification for that gap?

4. How would I describe the distance between our internal performance narrative and the performance reality that an independent external diagnostic would surface, and is that distance growing or closing?

5. What would need to change in how we communicate performance results at every level of the organisation to make radical transparency a genuine operating principle rather than a stated aspiration?

F. Questions about sustaining the reset over time

1. What are the specific mechanisms I have put in place to ensure that the accountability standards established in this reset continue to be applied consistently after the initial energy and visibility of the reset period has passed?

2. Where is the greatest risk of reversion to the previous cultural norm, and what early warning signals would tell me that reversion has begun before it becomes too embedded to address?

3. How am I building the internal leadership capability to sustain an accountable culture independently of my own presence and continued direct intervention?

4. What is the governance architecture that will surface accountability failures twelve months from now with the same speed and specificity that the reset's initial diagnostic did, and is that architecture genuinely in place?

5. In three years' time, what would I hope someone walking into this organisation would observe as the enduring legacy of the accountability reset we undertook today?

G. Questions for boards on the psychosocial governance obligation

1. Has the board explicitly acknowledged psychosocial risk as a governance obligation of equivalent standing to financial, operational, and reputational risk, and is that acknowledgement reflected in our risk framework, board charter, or governance policy documentation or does it remain an implicit assumption that has never been formally tested?

2. What psychosocial risk indicators are currently included in the reporting the board receives, and are those indicators-role clarity, grievance and complaint patterns, turnover concentration in specific teams or functions, and consistency of performance standard application- specific and current enough to provide genuine early warning of a developing accountability or cultural risk, or are they lagging, aggregated, or absent entirely?

3. If a regulator or plaintiff's counsel were to examine the board's oversight of psychosocial risk in this organisation over the past twelve months, what evidence would exist of active and informed governance and where would the gaps be most difficult to defend?

4. Where in this organisation are the conditions that the psychosocial legislation is specifically designed to address- specifically chronic role ambiguity, unaddressed under-performance, unresolved interpersonal conflict at a leadership level, or a pattern of complaints that has been managed rather than resolved- most likely to exist, and has the board directly and specifically asked that question of management?

5. What is the board's current mechanism for receiving independent assurance on the psychosocial health of the organisation that does not rely exclusively on the management reporting produced by the system it is being asked to assure, and if that mechanism does not yet exist, what is the plan and timeline for building it?

Closing Reflection — Chapter 8

The leader who stood on that stage in North America and told his team they had made a profit when they had made a loss was not a dishonest person. He was a good person operating inside a cultural norm that had quietly and over a long period of time made honest accountability feel less responsible than comfortable encouragement.

That is how accountability resets become necessary: not through a single catastrophic failure of integrity, but through the accumulated weight of individually understandable decisions that together produce a culture in which the truth about performance is no longer the default starting point for any conversation about it.

This is the inverse Discipline Dividend: the compound cost of accumulated avoidance, playing out in exactly the way that compound returns work in reverse. The longer the standard is not applied, the more expensive the reset. The earlier the line is held, the more the dividend compounds. The organisations that reset fastest and hold the line most consistently after the reset are the ones who understand, usually from having paid this cost once, that the Discipline Dividend is not a luxury of organisational health. It is a prerequisite of it.

Resetting that culture is hard, demanding, slow, and when it is done well, is one of the most genuinely satisfying things a leader can do. Because on the other side of the discomfort of honest standards clearly held, there is an organisation in which people know where they stand, know what matters, and can build genuine confidence in their own capability to meet the bar that has been set.

Based on my own experience, that is most definitely worth the effort.

Here is a space for your own reflection on this chapter. What resonated with you?

(Write your thoughts here)

____

____

____

____

____

CHAPTER 9

GROWING PEOPLE AT THE SPEED ORGANISATIONS ACTUALLY NEED

"Before you are a leader, success is all about growing yourself. When you become a leader, success is all about growing others."

—Jack Welch,
former Chairman and CEO, General Electric

Growth can't be rushed. And it won't work in the dark.

The organisations most frustrated by their people's capability gaps are almost always the same ones whose approach to closing those gaps is disconnected from the reality of the work those people are doing every day. They send their high-potentials to typically very expensive leadership programs that run for two days in a hotel conference room, or they invest in expensive coaches or online learning modules that sit untouched in a system that nobody logs into voluntarily. Alternatively, they bring in an external facilitator to run a workshop on strategic thinking for a group of people who will return on Monday morning to an environment that has been designed, in almost every structural way, to reward fast execution over thinking. And then, six months later, they express genuine puzzlement that despite their significant financial and resource investment, the capability needle has not moved in any meaningful direction.

I understand this frustration, and understand exactly how it happens, because I have personally been on both sides of it. In this chapter I will share what I have learned, through direct experience and more than a few expensive mistakes, about what capability development actually requires when it needs to happen at pace, and why the most powerful lever available to any leader is not a better training program, but a fundamentally different philosophy about the relationship between real work, real accountability, measurement, and practical learning.

The foundation of that personal philosophy was forged long before the North American transformation. It came from an earlier chapter of my career when I held a global human resources leadership role, delivering structural functional innovation in what became externally recognised as a uniquely commercial and sophisticated training architecture.

What made it sophisticated was not the content of the programs or the skill of the facilitators, though we were blessed that at that time both were genuinely excellent. It was unique in that the entire learning and development function was designed from the outset to be held to the same commercial standards of accountability as not only every other business unit in the organisation, but also to external training organisations.

This was enabled because in that company, the training function was reimagined not as a support service or an overhead. It was reinvented as a commercially viable service provider entity that had to generate profit, manage its costs, maintain high levels of (internal) customer satisfaction, justify its existence through measurable outcomes, and be independently audited on the quality of those outcomes several times a year.

When L&D is treated as a business, not a service

In most organisations I encounter, the learning and development function operates as an internal service provider that is evaluated primarily on the quality and delivery of its programs and the satisfaction of its participants. These are not irrelevant measures, but they are profoundly insufficient ones, because they measure inputs and experience rather than outputs and measurable commercial impact. An organisation can have exceptional participant satisfaction scores across its entire L&D portfolio and still be producing almost no durable capability and organisational improvement in the people going through it, and in many organisations that is precisely what is happening.

The organisation I am describing did something fundamentally different. It empowered me to treat the training function as a fully commercial internal business with its own profit and loss responsibility, its own key performance indicators tracked and published regularly, and its own accountability for the strategically-aligned commercial outcomes its work was intended to produce for the business. The training function did not receive a budget allocation and deploy it according to a learning strategy. It generated revenue on a fee-for-service basis by delivering capability outcomes that the operational business was prepared to pay for. The function was held accountable for those outcomes in the same rigorous and transparent way that any revenue-generating business unit in the organisation was held accountable for its commercial results: through robust guarantees and service level agreements.

The implications of that design principle were more profound than they might initially appear, and they were felt at every level of how the function operated. Trainers understood that they were not in the business of simply delivering programs; they were in the business of producing skilled people who could immediately perform in operational roles at the required standard. That distinction is not semantic. When the measure of a training intervention is whether participants enjoyed the experience and said positive things about it on a feedback form, the incentive is to design experiences that are engaging and comfortable.

When the measure is whether the people who went through the program are demonstrably more capable in their operational roles three months later, with that quantitative assessment made by agreed performance indicators and the managers who work alongside them every day rather than by the participants themselves, the incentive exists for HR to design interventions and assessments that actually change behaviour and build durable capability.

The audit and review architecture that underpinned this accountability was genuinely rigorous. Independent *external* reviewers assessed each training centre against a comprehensive set of benchmarks across four domains: trainer productivity, quality of training outcomes, the demonstrated skills of the trainers themselves, and the accuracy and integrity of documentation. The pass mark was high: seventy-five percent was the minimum for accreditation across every domain, and the assessment of quality of training outcomes used a deliberate triangulation methodology that drew data from three independent sources:

participant feedback; manager and team leader feedback on observed performance post-training; and objective knowledge and skills testing.

The reason for the triangulation was explicitly stated and was an intellectually honest design principle for training measurement. Data from a single source is inherently unreliable, and the most common single-source failure in training measurement is the over-reliance on participant satisfaction, which tells you whether people felt good about the experience rather than whether the experience changed their capability in measurable and operationally relevant ways.

The insight that made this architecture genuinely powerful was the discovery, confirmed consistently through the audit data, that the single most reliable predictor of training quality outcomes was not the content of the program, the accreditation of the trainer, or the participant satisfaction score. It was whether the manager or team leader of each participant had provided structured feedback on their post-training performance and whether the training function had proactively and systematically collected that feedback rather than relying on it to arrive of its own accord. Training centres that maintained a disciplined focus on obtaining manager feedback produced measurably better outcomes for new sales employees, stronger leadership development results, and earlier identification of skill gaps requiring corrective attention. Centres that allowed the feedback loop to lapse, even when their program quality was high, produced consistently weaker results. The conclusion was unambiguous: L&D without a closed feedback loop connecting training outcomes to operational performance is, at best, an incomplete investment, and at worst a comfortable fiction that allows the organisation to believe it is developing its people while the actual capability gap continues to compound.

The design and successful implementation of this rigorous L&D approach would not have happened without a skilled, passionate and capable co-designing team within the business and our highly skilled and pragmatic external HR advisors. We were all equally passionate about designing something new and meaningful. Ultimately, we wanted to prove we could move the dial significantly on organisational performance and were prepared to be held accountable for that.

What I carried forward from that experience is a set of convictions about learning and development that have proven consistently durable across very different organisational contexts, and that form the intellectual foundation of the approach I took in the North American transformation when I faced a capability gap that needed to be closed faster than any conventional training program could deliver.

The Executive Development Program (EDP): what it was and why it worked

The context matters here, so let me be specific. As previously mentioned, we were in the middle of a significant business recovery across three previously independent geographic regions, operating in a market that had been structurally disrupted by the events of September 11 and was still navigating the commercial and cultural aftermath of that disruption. As I described in Chapter 8, the accountability reset we were undertaking was demanding and at times deeply uncomfortable for the organisation.

What I was also acutely aware of, as that reset progressed and the new performance standards began to take hold, was that we had a capability gap that was going to become the binding constraint on the organisation's ability to sustain the recovery. We had a talented cohort of people who had enormous potential and genuine energy, but who had been operating in an environment that had not previously challenged them to think and lead at the level we now needed. The business needed them to grow, and it needed them to grow faster than any conventional development program I had seen was capable of delivering. We had identified significant gaps in succession for key roles and wanted to provide our internal teams with as much opportunity as possible to step up and fill those gaps.

So we built something different. We called it the Executive Development Program, and the core design principle was deliberately simple. If you want to grow future leaders, give them real leaders' problems to solve – not simulated versions of those problems, but live, urgent, genuinely strategic challenges that the business needed solved. Business problems and issues where the quality of the output could directly shape the direction of the organisation and where assessment was made with the same standard of evidence-based rigour, implementation credibility, and commercial defensibility that the senior leadership team applied to its own work.

The program grouped carefully selected high-potential participants into small teams of approximately six people each, drawn deliberately from across different functions and regions of the business so that no team was operating from a shared frame of reference or comfortable with an existing dynamic. Each team was assigned a specific, genuinely urgent strategic challenge: developing a flexible staffing formula for our retail businesses; building a multi-channel pricing strategy; creating an integrated customer retention framework; designing an effective staff retention approach for a specific business unit; and developing a site selection and growth strategy for the broader North American operation. These were not peripheral or low-stakes pieces of work. They were problems that the senior leadership team, including me, was actively trying to solve at the same time with limited bandwidth.

The teams were given a fixed and non-negotiable timeframe, external facilitation and rigorous independent assessment to ensure objectivity, and access to senior mentors within the business who could be consulted on a structured basis but who were explicitly not there to do the thinking for the teams. The team leader role rotated monthly, so every participant had to experience the accountability and pressure of leading a group through a difficult piece of work rather than simply contributing to one. They were required to brief me directly and regularly on their progress, which created an experience of accountability to senior leadership that most of them had never previously encountered in their careers.

Success was not assessed through participant satisfaction surveys or facilitator assessments of engagement. Drawing directly on the measurement discipline I had built in that earlier global HR role, I was determined that the assessment criteria would mirror the standard applied to actual commercial work: the rigour of the research methodology; the completeness of the options analysis; the quality and realistic application of the recommended strategy; the credibility of the proposed implementation plan; and the intellectual honesty with which the teams had tested their own assumptions rather than simply building a case for a predetermined conclusion. These were hard commercial measures of strategic thinking quality, not soft assessments of learning intent, and the participants understood from the outset that this was the standard against which their work and their potential would be evaluated.

What I was most deliberately not providing was a curriculum. There were no modules on strategic thinking, no workshops on stakeholder management, no sessions on how to build a business case. Those skills were developed not because they were taught but because the work demanded them. The experience of needing a skill urgently in the context of a real problem where the stakes are genuine is a categorically different learning experience from being introduced to that skill in a room where the stakes are abstract and the consequence of under-performance is a disappointing score on an assessment that nobody outside the program will ever see.

What happened as a result of that design validated everything I had come to believe about how adults actually develop capability, and confirmed what the audit data from my earlier global HR role had demonstrated with statistical consistency: that the quality of the feedback loop connecting learning to operational performance is the most powerful single variable in determining whether development investment produces genuine capability growth or the appearance of it.

Why real work is the most powerful learning environment available

There is a substantial body of research that supports what the EDP demonstrated in practice, even if most organisations have not yet translated its implications into the way they structure development. The widely cited 70-20-10 learning model, developed by Lombardo and Eichinger (1996) drawing on the earlier fieldwork of Morgan McCall and his colleagues at the Center for Creative Leadership, established that approximately seventy percent of meaningful professional development occurs through challenging assignments and real experience, twenty percent through developmental relationships and feedback, and only ten percent through formal training and education. That finding has been replicated and refined across decades of subsequent research, and the consistent conclusion is not that formal training has no value, but that *its value is almost entirely dependent on the quality and relevance of the real-work context in which it is applied.*

What the EDP was designed to exploit was precisely that seventy percent. The formal instruction was minimal and intentional. The program did not pretend that workshops and modules were the primary mechanism of growth. Instead it provided a carefully engineered real-work experience that was significantly more demanding, more cross-functional, and more strategically consequential than anything the participants would have encountered in their normal roles, combined with structured accountability, regular senior exposure, and the specific condition that made the learning most durable: the knowledge that the outcomes of their work genuinely mattered to the organisation they were part of.

That last element is, in my experience, the most under-estimated ingredient in the capability development equation. Adults learn most deeply when they understand that the problem in front of them is real, that their contribution to solving it matters, and that the accountability for doing so is genuinely theirs rather than a performance they are putting on for an assessor. The EDP created those conditions deliberately and comprehensively, and the development that resulted was visible, rapid, and in several cases genuinely transformative in terms of the confidence and capability of the individuals involved.

People who had previously operated within the comfortable boundaries of their own individual role discovered that they were capable of thinking at a level of complexity and ambiguity that neither they nor their managers had previously identified. The rotation of the team leader role produced a remarkably honest revelation of leadership strengths and gaps, because the pressure of actually leading a team through a difficult piece of work in front of peers with high expectations surfaces capability and its absence in ways that no 360-degree survey can replicate. And several individuals made the specific and observable transition that I regard as the most meaningful measure of real leadership development: from people who were waiting to be told what to think, to people who were generating original thinking of their own and backing it with evidence, analysis, and intellectual humility.

What most L&D investment actually buys

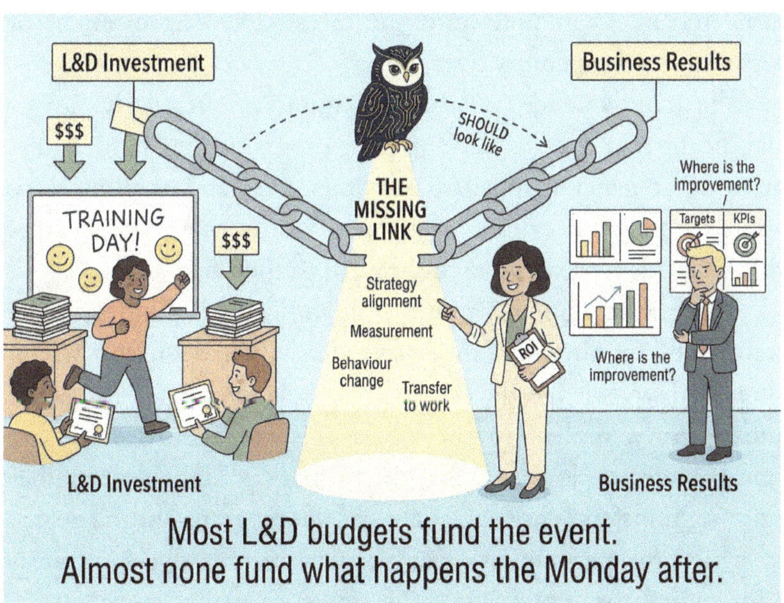

It might be uncomfortable to hear, but most organisational investment in learning and development produces results that are consistently disappointing relative to the financial and time resources committed.

Most L&D investment buys the appearance of development rather than development itself. It buys visible activity which often takes the form of programs attended, modules completed, facilitators engaged and certificates issued. That satisfies the organisational need to be seen to be investing in people without requiring the harder, slower, more ambiguous work of deliberately changing the conditions in which those people operate.

This is not a criticism of the individuals who design or deliver these programs, many of whom are genuinely skilled and dedicated professionals. It is a structural observation about the incentive architecture that most L&D functions operate within, which rewards the creation and delivery of learning content far more reliably than it rewards the measurable improvement of organisational capability over time.

The consequence is that organisations regularly invest significant resources in development programs that participants enjoy, that generate positive survey scores, and that produce approximately zero durable change in how those participants think, decide, or lead once they return to their own desks.

The research on this point is unambiguous. Studies of the transfer of training and more specifically, the degree to which skills and knowledge developed in formal learning settings are subsequently applied in the workplace, consistently find that transfer rates are low, and that the primary predictor of whether learning transfers is not the quality of the program but the degree to which the participant's work environment actively supports and requires the application of what was learned.

An organisation that sends its leaders to a program on courageous conversations and then returns them to a culture where the implicit norm is that difficult things are never said directly is not investing in development.

The EDP described above was expressly designed on the explicitly opposite premise: that with correctly structured training, the work environment is not external to, but rather the most integral development resource in the trainer's toolkit.

The four conditions that accelerate real capability development

Accelerated capability development requires four specific conditions to be present simultaneously. When all four are in place, the pace of development can be remarkable. When any one of them is absent, the others are significantly less effective, and formal training in the absence of all four is largely wasted.

The first condition is **genuine challenge at the edge of current capability.**

My experience is that development does not occur in the comfortable centre of what someone already knows how to do. It occurs at the boundary between what they can do with their current capability and what they cannot yet do without growing. The EDP created this condition deliberately by assigning participants to challenges that were meaningfully beyond their current experience, and by the design decision to make those challenges cross-functional, so that no participant could rely on their existing domain expertise as a substitute for the broader strategic and leadership thinking the program required. The relevant implication for leaders is simple and demanding: if the work you are giving your high-potential people does not regularly put them in situations where they are genuinely uncertain and stretched, you are not developing them at the pace the organisation needs, regardless of how many development or mentoring programs they attend.

The second condition is **accountability that is real and visible.** The most common reason that development experiences fail to produce durable capability growth is that the accountability attached to them is performative rather than genuine. Participants know, at some level, that the consequences of failure are limited and that the primary measure of success is engagement "theatre" and effort rather than outcome quality. The EDP addressed this by making the outcomes matter to the business in a way that was transparent to the participants from the outset. The problems they were solving were real, the senior (and global) leadership teams were watching – quite literally as they had to make their presentations to the Global Executive via video conferencing. They knew we would act on their recommendations, and the quality of their work would be directly visible to the people responsible for decisions about their future careers. That combination of genuine stakes and genuine visibility produced a quality of intellectual effort and personal accountability that can't be found through any theoretical development program, however well designed.

The third condition is **high-quality feedback that is close to the work and specific to the performance.** The feedback that produces the most durable development is not the annual performance review, the 360-degree survey result, or the end-of-program assessment. It is the specific, timely, honest observation delivered in direct proximity to the work it is about, by someone whose judgement the recipient respects and whose relationship with them is grounded in genuine mutual accountability rather than organisational courtesy.

The EDP provided this through the structure of regular presidential briefings, where I gave direct and specific feedback on the quality of the team's thinking and the clarity of their communication, and through the external facilitation that provided a genuinely independent assessment perspective. What made that feedback effective was not its sophistication but its specificity and its proximity. It landed close enough to the actual work that participants could immediately connect it to a decision they had made, an assumption they had relied on, or a moment in the team dynamic that they could recall and interrogate.

The fourth condition is **a genuine belief that growth is possible and expected.** This is the condition that is most frequently overlooked in capability development conversations and that is, in my experience, the most important of the four when it comes to the development of people who have been operating in environments where the implicit message has been that they are good enough for where they are but not quite ready for more.

One of the most powerful things a leader can communicate to a high-potential person who is not yet operating at the level you need is the specific and credible belief that they can.

Not as a motivational platitude or a performance management intervention, but as a genuine and informed assessment that you are prepared to back with the investment of a stretching opportunity and the ongoing support required to navigate it.

That specific combination, real opportunity plus genuine expressed confidence from a credible senior person, produces more rapid and durable capability development than any formal program I have ever designed or commissioned.

Strategy, measurement, and the missing link in most L&D investment

Capability development that is not explicitly connected to the strategic priorities and stated objectives of the organisation is not truly capability development: in reality, it is a welfare benefit.

This sounds harsh and I do not mean it dismissively, because learning and growth are intrinsically valuable and organisations have a real responsibility to invest in the development of their people for reasons that go beyond immediate commercial return. But the disconnection between learning and development investment and the strategic capability requirements of the organisation is one of the most expensive and preventable inefficiencies in modern business, and the leaders and boards who tolerate it are making a bad choice that compounds over time with very significant consequences.

The EDP was strategically connected by design and by necessity. The challenges the teams were working on were not selected because they would provide good learning experiences, though they did. They were selected because they were the most urgent and consequential strategic problems the business needed solved, and because solving them required exactly the capabilities: cross-functional strategic thinking, evidence-based analysis, structured implementation planning, disciplined team leadership under pressure, that the organisation needed its next generation of senior leaders to develop. At the end of the program, we very visibly implemented the recommendations and approach identified by the best groups, so they could see the direct outcomes of their learning impact the business transformation in real time.

The learning and the strategy were the same thing, not parallel activities that happened to occur simultaneously. That integration is what made the program both commercially valuable and developmentally powerful in a way that neither strand could have achieved independently.

The measurement architecture reinforced this connection in a fundamental way. Success was not assessed by participant satisfaction surveys or facilitator assessments of engagement. It was assessed by the quality of the strategic outputs the teams produced, measured against specific commercial criteria: the rigour of the research methodology; the completeness of the options analysis; the quality and appropriateness of the recommended strategy; and the credibility of the implementation plan and measurement framework. These were not soft measures of learning intent. They were hard measures of the quality of strategic thinking that, when applied to real business problems, produced real commercial outcomes. The participants understood from the outset that this was the standard, and that understanding shaped both the quality of their effort and the quality of their learning in ways that no softer assessment architecture could have produced.

What AI now makes possible in capability development

I want to spend a moment on something that genuinely excites me about the current environment for capability development, because it changes the equation in ways that were not available when I designed the EDP and which represent one of the most significant and under-exploited opportunities in modern leadership practice.

The four conditions I described earlier: genuine challenge, real accountability, high-quality specific feedback, and expressed belief in growth potential, have historically been expensive and time-consuming to create at scale, because all four depend on the direct involvement of experienced leaders who can design the right challenge, hold the accountability, provide the proximate feedback, and communicate the credible belief. Those leaders are scarce, their time is finite, and the one-to-one developmental attention that produces the most powerful growth has always been a resource that most organisations can provide to only a small proportion of their people at any given time.

AI changes that scarcity in ways that are already practically available and that are becoming more powerful with every iteration of the tools. Its ability to provide a genuinely rigorous, contextually relevant thinking partner that can stress-test analysis, challenge assumptions, surface the gaps in reasoning, and generate alternative perspectives at any hour and in any context is a capability development resource of a kind that simply did not exist before. Used well, it does not replace the human developmental relationship; it extends its reach and its frequency into the spaces between the conversations that experienced mentors and leaders can provide directly.

In my own advisory practice, and the organisations I work with, the greatest returns come when AI is used not as an answer machine but as a thinking partner in the specific day-to-day moments where thinking actually occurs:

- when a leader is working through a genuinely difficult strategic problem and uses AI to test their own reasoning before presenting it to a board,
- when a high-potential is building a business case and uses AI to identify and test the assumptions they have not yet examined,
- when a team is preparing for a consequential decision and uses AI to generate the strongest possible counter-argument to their preferred position.

These are not abstract applications. They are the specific moments in real work where the four conditions I described are most naturally present, and where the addition of a rigorous, available, non-judgemental AI thinking partner can materially accelerate the quality of the learning that those moments produce.

The integration of AI-enabled capability development into the strategic learning architecture of an organisation is one of the most commercially significant opportunities available to leaders and boards right now, and one that the majority of organisations are either ignoring entirely or engaging with at a level of superficiality that will not produce the outcomes they need.

Building a development architecture that connects genuine strategic challenges with real and measurable accountability, high-quality feedback close to the work, and AI-enabled thinking support in the moments that matter should not be a "one day" aspiration.

It is practically achievable today, and the organisations that build it deliberately will have a capability development advantage that compounds over time in exactly the way that the most valuable competitive advantages do.

The leader's role in growing people: what has not changed

I want to close this chapter with something that is in genuine danger of being lost in the current conversation about AI, technology, and the future of work, because it is easy in a period of rapid change to mistake the tools for the thing itself.

The most important element in any capability development architecture (more important than the design of the program, the quality of the assessment framework, the sophistication of the AI tools, or the rigour of the strategic connection) is the individual leader who chooses to invest genuine, sustained, personal attention in the development of a specific person.

Investment not through a program or a platform, but through the daily practice of holding someone to a standard that is slightly beyond their current capability, giving them the honest specific feedback that they need rather than the comfortable feedback that is easier to deliver, backing their potential with real opportunity before it is fully proven, and maintaining that investment through the inevitable periods of uncertainty and struggle that genuine growth always involves.

That practice has produced the most remarkable and most durable capability development in the people I have worked with and led. It does not scale easily, it is not measurable in the ways that boards and HR functions tend to prefer, and it requires a quality of leadership attention and emotional investment that is genuinely demanding. But its returns, in terms of the confidence, capability, and loyalty it produces in the people who experience it, are so far beyond what any formal program can deliver that the comparison is not really meaningful.

The EDP was not a perfect program, however it worked as well as it did because the people in it understood that the organisation's most senior leaders had made a personal, and credible commitment to their development and that the work they were being asked to do was not a test to be passed, but an investment to be honoured. That understanding changed the quality of their effort, the depth of their engagement, and ultimately the pace and durability of their growth in ways that no program design element could have produced on its own.

That is still true today, and it will remain true regardless of how sophisticated the AI tools available to support capability development become. The best professional development architecture in the world, without the human leader who is genuinely and personally committed to the growth of specific individuals within it, will produce competent development theatre rather than genuine capability growth.

And the most insightful leader in the world, without a development architecture that connects real challenge, real accountability for outcomes, and the best available analytical tools to the work of growing people, will produce sub-optimal developmental experiences that don't align to the speed at which organisations now need their people to grow.

The answer I believe, lies in both. The architecture and the human. The tools and the judgement. The structure and the relationship. Getting both right, at the same time, for a significant proportion of the people in your organisation, is hard. But it is among the most commercially valuable things a leadership team can do, and it is the standard to which the organisations that will lead their markets in the next decade are already beginning to hold themselves.

When you approach capability this way, you are not just "doing better development"; you are earning a very specific form of the Discipline Dividend. The same disciplined architecture you apply to expectations, accountability, and decision-making is now applied to how people grow. Over time, that discipline stops capability from being a happy accident and turns it into a compound return, with each cohort of leaders starting from a stronger base than the one before.

TOOLBOX — Chapter 9

Questions to examine your approach to growing people at the speed your organisation needs
Work through these questions honestly and with specific people, roles, and situations in mind. The most common failure in capability development planning is operating at a level of generality that feels productive but produces no change in how the organisation actually invests in growing its people.

A. Questions to diagnose the current development architecture

1. Is our current investment in learning and development explicitly connected to our most urgent strategic capability requirements, or are we investing in programs that were relevant to last year's strategy and this year's HR budget cycle?

2. What proportion of our development investment is creating genuine challenge at the edge of current capability, and what proportion is reinforcing skills and knowledge that our people already have?

3. Where in our organisation is the gap between the capability we need in the next twelve to twenty-four months and the capability we currently have most significant, and what is our specific, credible plan to close it?

4. How do we currently measure the commercial impact of our development investment, and are those measures capturing genuine capability growth or the appearance of it?

5. If I removed all formal L&D programs tomorrow and replaced them with nothing, which capability gaps would become critical within six months, and what does that tell me about where our development investment is actually adding value?

B. Questions about the four conditions for accelerated development

1. Which of my high-potential people are currently operating at the comfortable centre of their existing capability, and what would it take to move them to the genuine developmental edge?

2. Where in our organisation is real accountability attached to development experiences, and where is accountability performative, specifically where participants know that the stakes are limited and the primary measure is effort rather than outcome quality?

3. How close to the actual work is the feedback that our people receive on their performance, and how specific and honest is it when it arrives?

4. Where am I personally communicating a genuine and credible belief in the growth potential of specific individuals, and where am I withholding that belief until the capability is already proven, which is, of course, too late for it to serve a developmental function?

5. What is the most strategically urgent challenge in this organisation right now that could simultaneously serve as a powerful development experience for a high-potential team, and what is preventing me from designing that experience?

C. Questions about the connection between strategy and development

1. Could I clearly describe, to a sceptical board member, the specific connection between our current L&D investment and our most critical strategic capability requirements for the next three years?

2. Where are we investing in development that is disconnected from strategic priority and what is the honest reason for that disconnection?

3. What capabilities does the organisation need its next generation of senior leaders to have that its current generation of senior leaders does not consistently demonstrate, and does our development architecture explicitly address that gap?

4. How are the strategic challenges the organisation is currently facing being used as development opportunities for the people who need to grow, and where are we solving those challenges exclusively at a senior level rather than using them as the most powerful development resource available to us?

5. In three years' time, what do we want to be able to say about how the capability of this organisation's leadership pipeline has changed, and is our current development investment on a credible path to produce that outcome?

D. Questions about the leader's personal role in development

1. Which specific individuals in my organisation am I personally and actively committed to developing, and what does that commitment look like in practice beyond their inclusion in a formal program?

2. Where am I giving honest, specific, close-to-the-work feedback on development, and where am I defaulting to the comfortable feedback that is easier to deliver but less useful to receive?

3. What opportunities have I created in the past six months that stretched a high-potential person beyond their current proven capability, and what did I observe as a result?

4. Where is my own leadership behaviour modelling the kind of learning orientation, intellectual humility, and growth commitment that I am asking of the people I am responsible for developing?

5. What is the single most important thing I could do differently in the next ninety days to meaningfully accelerate the

capability development of the people who matter most to the future of this organisation?

E. Questions about AI and the future of capability development
1. Where in the flow of real work could AI-enabled thinking support most meaningfully accelerate the development of my people, and am I actively creating the conditions and the permission for them to use it that way?
2. How am I helping my people distinguish between using AI as a thinking partner that challenges and extends their judgement, and using it as an answer machine that produces outputs they do not need to understand or defend?
3. What would a development architecture look like that combined the real-challenge design of the EDP with AI-enabled thinking support at the moments in real work where genuine learning occurs, and what would it take to build that in this organisation?
4. Where are my people already using AI in ways that are accelerating their development, and where are they using it in ways that are substituting for development rather than accelerating it?
5. In five years, what do I expect the best organisations in our sector to be doing to develop capability faster than their competitors, and what would it take to start building that architecture now rather than then?

Closing Reflection — Chapter 9

The EDP produced leaders who went on to progress in their careers and run significant parts of that business, not because it was the most sophisticated program ever designed, but because it treated the people in it as capable of contributing to the organisation's most important and pressing challenges before they had fully proven they could and then created the conditions for that belief to become justified.

That is the essence of developmental leadership. Not the management of capability risk, or the warm and fuzzy generic learning, but the deliberate and sustained investment in what people can become, backed by real opportunity, honest feedback, and the kind of expressed confidence that makes people genuinely want to rise to the level of the belief placed in them.

The organisations that grow the best people, fastest, are the ones whose leaders understand that growing people and running the business are not competing demands on the same finite resource. They are, when done well, the same activity.

Capability built through disciplined, architecturally integrated development pays exactly the same compound return as discipline in accountability, culture, and decision-making.

The Discipline Dividend is not domain-specific.

It compounds across every dimension of the organisation simultaneously. The leaders who understand this invest in capability the same way they hold the accountability line – consistently, architecturally, and without allowing the comfortable alternative to substitute for the rigorous one.

*Here is a space for your own reflection on this chapter. What reso-
nated with you?*

(Write your thoughts here)

____

____

____

____

____

____

CHAPTER 10

THE DECISION PLAYBOOK: BUILDING THE ARCHITECTURE OF BETTER DECISIONS

"Plans are worthless, but planning is everything."
—Dwight Eisenhower,
34th President of the United States

By this point in the book, a fairly clear picture of the kind of leader I am has likely formed, and it is, I acknowledge, a picture that may be slightly exhausting in its consistency.

Direct, pragmatic, commercially focused, and genuinely committed to the people and organisations I work with.

Allergic to theatre. Repulsed by politics and narcissistic power plays. Extremely comfortable with discomfort and with solving problems, and on a good day, capable of driving meaningful, lasting change.

That is the highlight reel, anyway.

But if I am going to write a book about accountability, intellectual honesty requires a confession: I have also made some genuinely poor decisions along the way.

Not the dramatic, headline-grabbing kind that end careers in flames, but the quieter, more insidious kind, specifically the ones that came from a blind spot in my own decision-making that I did not recognise nearly as quickly as I should have, and which I then proceeded to repeat, just to be certain.

In retrospect, those decisions have cost me, and the people around me, more than they needed to.

As for my poor personal decisions, they could comfortably fill another book, possibly a trilogy. For everyone's sake, they will remain unwritten.

The professional ones all followed the same pattern, and it is that pattern and how I eventually learned to break it, that anchors this chapter.

The flaw I kept repeating

I am, by my own assessment and by the consistent feedback of people I trust and respect, genuinely strong at communicating across large and diverse organisations. I can bring teams together with energy and alignment around a transformation or a business journey in ways that produce real and visible momentum and successfully drive significant transformation. I have done it multiple times, across different organisations, different cultures, and different degrees of commercial difficulty, and the results have been real.

What I am not good at, and what some people who have worked with and around me have accurately described in considerably more direct terms, is managing upwards – engaging the critical stakeholders above me with the same intentionality, patience, and strategic investment that I bring to the people I am leading with and below me.

My brain, when I am in the middle of a significant transformation and the operational momentum is building and the team is engaged and the results are beginning to move, does not naturally orient toward the senior stakeholders who are not yet fully on board. My internal assessment in those moments is characteristically direct and characteristically unhelpful: they just do not get it. And my natural response to that assessment is to be impatient with what feels like political noise and to keep moving rather than slow down to better align and bring those stakeholders fully onto the journey.

I can identify three separate points in my executive career, across different organisations, and different roles (including holding CEO positions) where I misread the room in precisely this way. I misjudged the implications of proceeding through a critical juncture without the full engagement and genuine buy-in of the stakeholders whose support was not optional, whatever my internal assessment of their understanding suggested. In each case, it ended badly. For me and for people around me. And I am honest enough with myself to acknowledge that there were probably further instances where the consequences were contained only by the commercial results I was delivering simultaneously; a form of organisational tolerance that I should not have been relying on and that was never going to be unlimited.

I have also on occasion, been far too blindingly loyal to, and trusting of, leaders above me who didn't hold the same level of integrity and values alignment as I did. Each and every time I did this, it also ended very badly for me.

What I discovered, through the slow and sometimes painful process of reflecting on those experiences, is that every one of them shared a specific and identifiable failure in the decision-making architecture. Not just in the quality of the decisions themselves, but in the process by which those decisions were pressure-tested, communicated, and translated into genuine alignment across the people whose understanding and commitment were essential to making them work. And that failure was not unique to me. It is, in fact, one of the most common and most costly structural failures in the decision-making processes of talented, experienced, and commercially capable leaders across every sector and organisational scale.

Why decision architecture matters more than decision talent

The most dangerous assumption in most organisations' approach to decision-making is that the quality of decisions is primarily a function of the quality of the individual leaders making them. It follows from this assumption that the path to better decisions is better leaders; more experienced, more analytically capable, better trained in the frameworks and tools of strategic thinking. And there is something to that argument, but it is not the primary lever. It is the environment in which they are making decisions.

The research on this point is consistent and humbling. Studies of decision-making in organisations consistently find that individual intelligence, domain expertise, and leadership experience are *surprisingly weak predictors of decision quality* once the social, structural, and political dynamics of the decision-making environment are accounted for. Smart people in poorly designed decision environments make poor decisions with genuine confidence. And the confidence is not incidental. It is a product of the same cognitive architecture that makes them effective in many other domains, now operating without the structural checks that would surface the gaps in their reasoning before those gaps produce consequences.

What distinguishes the organisations that make consistently better decisions is not the average capability of their leaders. It is the architecture within which those leaders make decisions, specifically the structures, processes, norms, and disciplines that determine who is in the room, how options are generated and evaluated, how assumptions are tested, how dissent is structured and heard, and how commitment is secured in a way that preserves genuine uncertainty rather than suppressing it in the name of alignment.

That architecture does not emerge naturally from good intentions or talented people. It has to be designed, maintained, and defended against the very human pressures that consistently erode it.

The six most common decision-making failure modes

In Chapter 6, I described the judgement gap: the progressive and largely invisible degradation in the quality of organisational decision-making that occurs when metric drift, narrative distortion, and the normalisation of comfortable ambiguity are allowed to compound over time. I want to build on that diagnostic here by naming the six most common structural failure modes in decision-making that I observe consistently, because the architecture of better decisions requires understanding specifically what it is being built to prevent.

1. Premature convergence

This is the tendency of decision-making groups to reach consensus before the full option space has been genuinely explored. This is one of the most consistently under-estimated failure modes, because it feels like efficiency and alignment at the moment it occurs.

The group has coalesced around an early-identified answer, the energy in the room is positive, and continuing to generate alternatives feels like prolonging a process that has already found its destination. What is actually happening is that the social dynamics of the group, namely the influence of the most senior voice, the desire of participants to be seen as constructive rather than obstructive, the cognitive comfort of having a clear path forward, have closed down the option space before the most important alternatives have been adequately considered.

Some of the most expensive decisions I have seen made in boardrooms and executive teams were not wrong because the chosen option was obviously bad. They were wrong because a better option was never seriously considered.

2. Assumption invisibility

This is the failure to surface and test the assumptions on which a decision is built before those assumptions are embedded in the decision's architecture. Every significant decision rests on a set of assumptions about the future state of the world, the behaviour of competitors and customers, the capabilities and resources of the organisation, and the reliability of the information being used to evaluate options. When those assumptions are not explicitly named, they cannot be tested. Decisions built on invisible assumptions are structurally fragile in ways that only become visible when the world fails to cooperate with the assumptions that were never examined. The discipline of asking, before any significant decision is finalised, "what would have to be true for this decision to be correct, and how confident are we that it is true?" is one of the most powerful and most consistently absent practices in organisational decision-making.

3. Authority gradient distortion

This is the phenomenon I described in my own professional failure above, where the presence of a more senior voice in a decision-making group changes the quality of the contributions from less senior participants in ways that are invisible to everyone including the senior person whose presence is causing the distortion.

People do not generally decide to withhold their genuine assessment in the presence of authority. They do so automatically, often without awareness, through the entirely rational social calculation that the cost of being visibly wrong in front of a senior person is higher than the cost of quietly deferring to a view that may itself be wrong.

The result is decision-making groups that appear to be engaged in genuine deliberation while actually engaged in sophisticated social performance, and the most senior person in the room is typically the least aware that this is happening. I have witnessed this dynamic in meeting rooms far more often than many other decision-making flaws.

4. Timeline compression

This is the systematic erosion of decision quality that occurs when
the time available for deliberation is compressed by urgency, real
or constructed, to the point where the process that would surface
the second-order consequences of a decision cannot be completed
before the decision must be made. There is genuine urgency in
organisational life, and not every decision can or should be sub-
jected to an extended deliberative process.

Often though, the urgency that compresses decision quality is
the result of kicking the can down the road (figuratively speaking)
until it can be kicked no more, or of a cultural norm that con-
flates fast decisions with decisive leadership.

Decisions made under constructed urgency carry the full
risk of decisions made under genuine urgency without the
justification.

5. Dissent suppression

This is the cultural dynamic in which genuine disagreement,
doubt, or concern about a proposed decision is perceived to potentially be too costly by the person holding those views. This is the
failure mode that my own experience most directly illustrates: the
critical stakeholders I was not adequately engaging were, in some
respects, the organisational equivalent of the dissenting voice I
had not built a genuine architecture for hearing.

Their concerns were not absent from the situation. They were
present but not surfaced in a way that could be incorporated
into the decision architecture before commitment was made.
The consequence was not that the decision was always wrong,
but that its implementation was far more fragile than it needed
to be, because the people whose understanding and buy-in were
essential to making it work had not genuinely provided either.

6. Commitment without alignment

This situation, deeply familiar to anyone who has led a significant transformation, is where a decision appears to have been made and agreed by the relevant parties but where the quality of the commitment varies so dramatically across those parties that the decision is effectively unmade in implementation.

This is perhaps the most insidious failure mode of all, because it is invisible in the decision-making room. It only becomes visible in the gap between what was agreed and what is subsequently enacted, at which point the cost of re-engaging the alignment question is significantly higher than it would have been at the point of decision. It is also, in my direct experience, the failure mode most commonly produced by leaders who are strong at driving operational momentum but less disciplined about the patient, politically nuanced work of building genuine alignment across all stakeholders.

The decision architecture framework

The practical architecture of better decisions is not complicated, but it is disciplined, and the discipline is exactly what makes it difficult to sustain in organisations under the real pressures of operational pace, leadership hierarchy, and the entirely human preference for arriving at clarity quickly.

The first element is deliberate option generation. Before any significant decision is evaluated, the group responsible for making it should explicitly generate a minimum of three to four genuinely distinct options, including – at minimum – one that challenges the framing of the decision itself. The instinct to move quickly to evaluation of the preferred option is strong and should be explicitly resisted until the option space has been genuinely explored. The most useful structural question at this stage is not "how do we assess these options?" but "what options have we not yet considered, and why not?"

The second element is explicit assumption mapping. For each option under consideration, the group should explicitly name the two or three most critical assumptions on which that option's viability rests, and then honestly assess the evidence for each. This is not an abstract analytical exercise. It is a discipline of intellectual honesty that surfaces the places where a decision is being driven by hope or habit rather than by evidence. That makes the decision's vulnerability to specific kinds of environmental change visible before rather than after commitment.

The third element is structured dissent. Every significant decision-making process should include an explicit mechanism for surfacing dissenting perspectives that does not require the individual holding those perspectives to assume the full social cost of

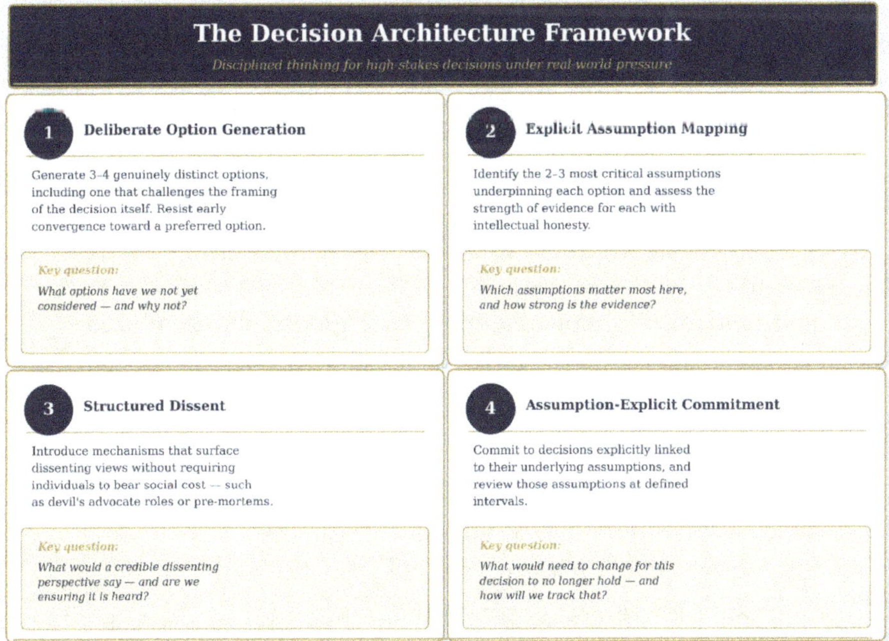

expressing them. This can take the form of a formally assigned devil's advocate role, a pre-mortem exercise in which the group is asked to assume the decision has failed and work backwards to identify why, or a structured private polling of individual assessments before group discussion begins. The specific mechanism matters less than the genuine commitment to creating a space where the inconvenient perspective is sought rather than tolerated.

The fourth element is assumption-explicit commitment. When a decision is finalised, the commitment to it should be explicitly conditional on the assumptions it rests on, and those conditions should be documented and reviewed at defined intervals rather than assumed to remain valid until a problem forces them back into view. This is not the same as hedging or failing to commit. It is the recognition that organisational decisions are made in conditions of genuine uncertainty, and that building in explicit assumption review is a form of intellectual rigour rather than a form of organisational timidity.

The communication architecture: the stage that most decisions skip

I want to spend time on something that is as consequential as any element of the decision process itself. Once a decision has been made, regardless of how disciplined the process that produced it was, the quality of the decision's implementation is overwhelmingly determined by the quality and intentionality of the communication architecture that follows it.

This is where my own failure mode was most acute, and where I have done the most subsequent thinking. What I discovered through those three experiences I described at the opening of this chapter is that I was treating the communication of a significant decision as a relatively straightforward operational task: tell the relevant people; explain the rationale; secure their agreement; move forward. What I had not understood is that the communication of a significant decision to the people whose understanding and genuine alignment is required to implement it successfully is itself a complex, multi-stage, multi-channel process that requires as much deliberate architecture as the decision-making process that preceded it.

The simple framework I have developed, centres on four dimensions of effective strategic communication which produce a qualitatively different quality and power of organisational alignment.

The first dimension is **the WHY**: the reason the decision has been made, explained in terms of the strategic and commercial context that makes it necessary and the problem this decision solves for. People who understand why a decision was made (regardless of whether they agree with it specifically) are categorically more likely to implement it faithfully, adapt it intelligently when conditions change, and advocate for it credibly to the stakeholders within their own sphere of influence. People who have been told what the decision is without being told why will implement it literally, fail to adapt it appropriately, and provide no advocacy at all when the inevitable questions arise from those around them.

The second dimension is **the WHAT**: the specific outcomes, behaviours, and performance indicators that will tell the organisation whether the implementation of the decision is producing the results it was designed to produce. Without explicit WHAT, measurement defaults to activity rather than outcome, and the organisation can be very busy implementing a decision in ways that are not producing the intended result for a considerable period before anyone has the organisational permission to point out the problem.

The third dimension is **the HOW**: the specific process by which the decision will be implemented, with sufficient clarity that the people responsible for acting on it do not have to infer, improvise, or seek clarification on the elements that are genuinely within the control of the decision-makers to specify. Ambiguity in the HOW is not flexibility; it is a transfer of decision-making burden to the people least equipped with the context to make those calls well.

The fourth dimension is **the WHEN**: the explicit timeline, milestones, and review points that create the accountability architecture for implementation, and that ensure the decision does not become the latest in a long series of organisational commitments that were genuinely intended and never genuinely delivered. In my experience, the absence of an explicit WHEN is the single most reliable predictor of a decision that will not be implemented at the

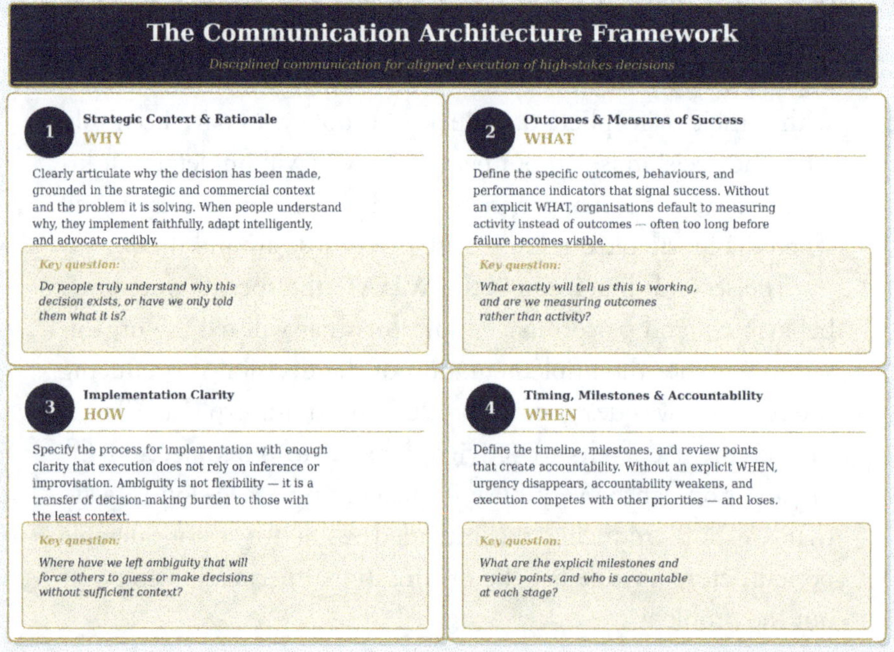

standard required. Without a timeline there is no accountability, and without accountability the urgency of implementation competes with every other priority in the organisation until it loses.

The framework is deceptively simple. Its power lies entirely in the discipline with which it is applied and specifically in two elements that most organisations consistently underestimate: sequencing and repetition.

What makes this framework an architecture rather than a checklist is the attention paid to sequencing and repetition across multiple channels. The critical mistake most organisations make in communicating significant decisions is communicating them once, through a single channel (usually a written announcement or an all-hands meeting) and then assuming the messaging will be passed on with the same effectiveness thus treating communication as complete.

The research on how adults absorb and retain information is aligned on this point, and my own decades of experience in change management and transformation confirm it: people need to hear important messages multiple times, through different channels, in language calibrated to their specific context and role, and positioned in a consistent way, before the message genuinely lands in a way that changes behaviour rather than simply generating awareness. A single town hall meeting is not communication. It is the beginning of communication, and the organisations that treat it as the end are consistently surprised when the implementation of their carefully considered decisions fails to produce the outcomes those decisions were designed to achieve.

There is one other critical element in the effective delivery and absorption of strategic decisions, and the best way I know to illustrate it is through a game most of you will have played as a child: Chinese whispers.

The rules of the game are simple. A large group sits in a circle. One person is given a specific, detailed message and whispers it to the next person, but once only. Each person then passes what they heard to the next, until the final person repeats the message aloud. The result, without exception, is that the original message has been so thoroughly distorted in its journey around the room that it bears almost no resemblance to what was said at the start.

During my North American transformation, I learned this lesson very painfully in the first six months. I relied on all of the leadership layers to repeat the agreed messaging and communication of our transformation decisions and actions throughout their divisions and geographies with urgency. Inevitably, the messages were distorted and significantly diluted, thus slowing down our adoption and progress. The reasons are obvious upon reflection. Leaders have varying capability with difficult messages, varying capabilities in handling objections or questions, and they often have varying levels of commitment to the strategy, approach or organisation.

At the six-month mark, when it became clear we were not getting the traction needed to execute effectively, it became undeniable: unless each person could hear the key messages – specifically a consistent version of the WHY, WHAT, HOW, and WHEN directly from me – the distortion would continue to impede our progress.

From that point on, despite the technology challenges back then, I personally delivered all key messages on strategy, decisions, plans and expectations to every level of the organisation from top to bottom in a way that aligned and engaged our teams in an incredible way. Not just in one channel, but the same messages from me verbally, in person, and in writing repeated many times to ensure absorption and understanding.

The difference in traction was breathtaking. This approach did not absolve the leaders from continuing to repeat and communicate the messages to their teams, but it made it much easier for them. I effectively gave them the "script" and template of how to do it effectively, in a way that was entirely aligned to my own messaging, instead of relying on them to communicate the message down through the organisations in their own way.

Another important lesson concerned the sequencing of the communication of decisions: ensuring the appropriate levels of leadership knew and understood and had personal "buy in" of the decisions ahead of any mass communication roll-outs.

This sequencing was critical to generating genuine ownership and accountability at every level. On the occasions when rushed communication meant I skipped that step with key leaders, both ownership and accountability became casualties, visible in the gap between what was agreed in the room and what was actually delivered in the field.

The role of AI in decision support

The practical contribution AI can make to the decision architecture I have described is already available and is being significantly under-utilised in most of the organisations I work with.

In the option generation stage, AI can expand the option space beyond the boundaries of what the group's existing mental models would naturally produce, by drawing on patterns from adjacent industries, historical analogues, and analytical frameworks that the group has not considered. This is not a replacement for human strategic judgement: the filtering and contextualisation of those options requires exactly the kind of experienced judgement that AI cannot replicate. But it is a genuine and practically available antidote to the premature convergence failure mode, because it introduces perspectives that the group's social and cognitive dynamics would not naturally generate.

In the assumption mapping stage, I have personally used AI to effectively stress-test the assumptions underlying each option by rapidly generating scenarios under which those assumptions fail, identifying the conditions that would most significantly change the risk profile of the decision, and surfacing historical analogues where similar assumptions proved to be the critical failure point. Again, the human judgement required to assess the relevance of those analogues and the credibility of those scenarios is not replaced, however it is better informed.

In the structured dissent stage of this framework, AI used as a thinking partner by individuals before a group process begins, can produce a quality of independent pre-analysis that significantly improves the perspectives brought into the room. This is in large part because the person who has pressure-tested their own thinking against a rigorous AI interlocutor in the hours before a significant meeting arrives with a much more thorough perspective than the person who has relied on their existing mental model alone.

What AI cannot do in the decision architecture is carry the relational and political work of genuine alignment: the direct, honest, one-to-one conversations that are required to understand and address the concerns of critical stakeholders who are not yet on board. That work, as my own experience confirms, cannot be delegated or substituted.

It requires the human leader to make themselves genuinely available to the perspectives of people whose understanding and commitment they need, in a way that is patient, specific, and genuinely curious rather than performatively consultative. No AI capability currently available or on the visible horizon changes or can fulfill that requirement.

The decision was made. Nobody told the people who had to carry it out.

What to do on Monday morning

I want to close the substantive argument of this chapter with something deliberately practical, because a playbook that does not produce changed behaviour is a framework, not a tool.

First, before your next significant decision, write down the three most critical assumptions on which your current preferred option rests, and ask yourself honestly what evidence you have for each. Not what you believe, or what your experience suggests, or what the team has generally agreed: what reliable evidence you have. The gap between what you believe and what you can evidence is the structural vulnerability of the decision.

Second, identify the critical stakeholders whose genuine alignment is required for the implementation of your next major decision to succeed, and ask yourself honestly whether you have invested the same quality of communication and engagement with each of them that you have invested in the people you are leading operationally. If the answer is no, the communication architecture of the decision is incomplete regardless of the quality of the decision itself.

Third, introduce a structured dissent mechanism into your next significant group decision-making process. Try a pre-mortem of ten minutes. Asking the group to assume the decision has failed two years from now and to work backwards to identify why, will surface more genuine risk assessment than most formal analytical processes, because it gives people organisational permission to voice the concerns they already hold but have not yet expressed.

Fourth, before communicating a significant decision, map its WHY, WHAT, HOW, and WHEN explicitly, and design the communication architecture with the same deliberateness you applied to the decision itself. Identify which channels, which messengers, and which sequencing will produce genuine understanding and alignment across the full range of people whose behaviour needs to change for the decision to produce its intended outcome.

Fifth, build assumption review into the implementation governance of every significant decision you make. Schedule the first review at ninety days, ask explicitly whether the critical assumptions on which the decision was built remain valid, and give yourself and your team organisational permission to adapt the decision's implementation on the basis of what you learn. The decision that cannot be adapted in the light of new evidence is not a good decision. It is a sign of poor leadership.

It is a sign of commitment to a process over commitment to an outcome. The discipline of better decisions is not dramatic. It is architectural, repeated, and quiet.

And like all discipline applied architecturally over time, it compounds into an organisation that makes fewer catastrophic decisions, wastes less time and resource reversing them, and builds the kind of institutional decision quality that becomes a genuine competitive advantage. That is the Discipline Dividend in the boardroom. It is unglamorous, non-negotiable, and among the highest-returning investments a leadership team can make.

TOOLBOX — Chapter 10

Questions to build the architecture of better decisions

A. Questions on option generation
1. How many genuinely distinct options did we consider before converging on this decision, and were any of those options a genuine challenge to the framing of the decision itself?
2. What options have we not considered, and what is the honest reason for not considering them — analytical elimination or social and political convenience?
3. Who in this process has the most to lose from the options we have not considered, and have we genuinely heard their perspective?
4. Where is our option generation most constrained by our existing mental models, and what would it take to expand beyond those constraints?
5. If this decision were being made by a leader with no prior investment in the current direction, what options would they consider that we have not?

B. Questions on assumption testing
1. What are the three most critical assumptions on which our preferred option rests, and what specific evidence supports each of them?
2. Under what conditions would each of those assumptions fail, and what would the consequence for the decision be if they did?

3. Where are we relying on belief, experience, or organisational consensus rather than current and specific evidence?

4. What would have to be true about the external environment for this decision to be significantly wrong, and how confident are we that those conditions do not currently apply?

5. What is the assumption we are least willing to test, and what does our unwillingness to test it tell us?

C. Questions on dissent and group dynamics

1. Who in this decision-making group holds the most genuinely dissenting perspective, and have they expressed it fully and been genuinely heard?

2. What is the authority gradient in this decision-making group, and what effect is it having on the quality and honesty of contributions from less senior participants?

3. If we ran a pre-mortem on this decision right now, assuming it has failed in two years and working backwards, what would the group identify as the most likely cause of failure?

4. Where in this process have I observed people deferring to authority rather than expressing genuine assessment, and what does that tell me about the quality of the deliberation?

5. What would a genuinely independent external perspective on this decision surface that our internal process has not?

D. Questions on commitment and alignment

1. Who are the critical stakeholders whose genuine understanding and commitment are required for this decision's implementation to succeed, and do I have honest evidence that they genuinely hold both?

2. Where is the commitment in this process performative rather than genuine, and what is driving the gap between the two?

3. What are the specific conditions under which each critical stakeholder's commitment might erode, and what is my plan for managing those conditions?

4. Have I had a direct, honest, private conversation with each critical stakeholder about their concerns, or have I relied on group process to surface and address dissent that group process is structurally unable to surface and address?

5. What would the critical stakeholders I have engaged with least say about this decision if asked privately, and how does that assessment compare with what they have expressed in the formal process?

E. Questions on communication architecture

1. Have I communicated the WHY of this decision; the genuine strategic and commercial context that makes it necessary, as clearly and specifically as I have communicated the WHAT?

2. Does every person responsible for implementing this decision have a clear and specific understanding of the HOW; what they are expected to do, by when, to what standard?

3. Have I defined the WHAT of this decision in terms of outcomes and behaviours rather than activities, and is that definition specific enough to be meaningfully measured?

4. What is the explicit WHEN architecture; the milestones, review points, and accountability mechanisms that will ensure this decision is implemented at the required standard rather than gradually deprioritised under the pressure of competing demands?

5. How many times, across how many channels, and in what sequence will the critical messages of this decision reach the people whose behaviour needs to change for it to produce

its intended outcome and is that plan genuinely adequate to the scale of the change required?

F. Questions on AI-assisted decision-making

1. Where in this decision process could AI have expanded the option space, stress-tested assumptions, or generated structured dissent in ways that our internal process did not?

2. Am I using AI as a genuine thinking partner that challenges and extends my reasoning, or as a tool for producing outputs that confirm my existing direction?

3. What would a rigorous AI-assisted pre-mortem of this decision surface, and am I willing to run one before committing?

4. Where are my people using AI in their own decision preparation, and is that usage producing better-informed perspectives or better-packaged versions of existing ones?

5. What decision support architecture would I want to have in place in twelve months, and what would it take to start building it now?

Closing Reflection — Chapter 10

The three professional failures I described at the opening of this chapter had one thing in common that I now regard as the most important single insight in my approach to decision-making. They were not failures of capability or commitment. They were failures of architecture and specifically, the failure to build a genuine process for hearing, engaging, and incorporating the perspectives of the people whose understanding and alignment were not optional components of the decisions' success.

The decisions themselves, in each case, were not obviously wrong. Several of them were, in their core strategic or commercial logic, sound. What made them produce bad outcomes was not the quality of the thinking that went into making them, but the insufficiency of the architecture built around making them well, particularly the absence of genuine dissent mechanisms, the under-investment in critical stakeholder alignment, and the communication architecture that assumed understanding would follow announcement rather than requiring the patient, repeated, multi-channel work of genuinely building it.

The discipline of better decisions is not primarily an analytical skill. It is an architectural one. And like all architecture, it requires deliberate design, regular maintenance, and the willingness to defend its integrity against the very human pressures that will consistently push toward the shortcuts that feel like efficiency but produce the failures that feel, in retrospect, like they should have been entirely avoidable.

Because in reality, they were.

*Here is a space for your own reflection on this chapter. What reso-
nated with you?*

(Write your thoughts here)

THE CULTURE PLAYBOOK: BUILDING THE ENVIRONMENT WHERE ACCOUNTABILITY BECOMES THE NORM

"Culture isn't just one aspect of the game; it is the game. In the end, an organisation is nothing more than the collective capacity of its people to create value."

—Lou Gerstner,
former Chairman and CEO, IBM

Culture isn't what you put on the wall.
It's what you tolerate on a Tuesday afternoon.

"Culture" is, without doubt, one of the most misunderstood, loosely defined, and commonly tossed-around words in our workplaces. That may seem an unfair opening, but over my career I have heard the phrase "we have a great culture" used generously by leaders to describe their own organisations. Despite aspirational mission and values statements plastered across meeting room walls, unfortunately I have often observed clear and consistent evidence that those statements bore absolutely no resemblance to the behaviours and actions of the leaders and individuals walking the very same corridors.

In some cases, I have witnessed a complete and total disconnect between every single element of the meeting room culture map and the lived reality of the organisation it claimed to describe. The contradiction is hard to miss.

Let us be honest about something. Every CEO and board want to believe their culture is healthy, and many take genuine pride in the belief (rightly or wrongly) that their culture is unique and special.

How many times have you heard a CEO say: "Our culture really sucks! Working here is genuinely terrible"? I would hazard a guess: not often. And yet the gap between the culture organisations describe and the culture they actually operate is one of the most consistent and costly structural failures I encounter in advisory work across every sector, every size, and every degree of organisational sophistication.

The truest indication of organisational culture is not the values statement, not the engagement survey result, and not the culture narrative in the annual report.

In reality, it is simply the sum of what an organisation consistently tolerates, rewards, and models. The leaders who build genuinely high-performance cultures are not the ones with the most compelling vision or the most sophisticated culture frameworks.

They are the ones most disciplined, most authentic, and most consistent in the daily practice of holding the line between what the culture says it stands for and what it actually permits.

The whiteboard that changed the conversation

In an advisory engagement with a large manufacturing business, I encountered what I described above: a clear and visible disconnect between stated cultural values and the daily reality of how the organisation operated. When I surfaced this observation, I received the pushback I have come to expect: not aggressive, but genuinely uncertain. The leadership team did not experience themselves as operating in contradiction to their stated values. They simply had not examined the gap with any rigour.

So we did a simple whiteboard exercise. Four columns. In the first, we listed each of the organisation's stated values and cultural norms. In the second, we wrote what behaviours each value would require in practice to be genuinely true, specifically what it would actually look like if someone were living that value rather than endorsing it. In the third column, we wrote how each of those behaviours was monitored and measured in the organisation. In the fourth, we asked each leader to rate on a scale of one to ten how consistently they and their teams actually modelled the behaviour required or could observe it in practice across their teams.

The result was instructive in a way that no HR engagement survey had been. The second column revealed that even when leaders could articulate a cultural attribute, they had significant difficulty identifying how it could or should practically be exhibited in day-to-day leadership behaviour. The third column was worse. The response rate to "How is this behaviour monitored or measured?" was zero across every single cultural attribute. Not one of the values the organisation aspired to was measurable or monitored in any form. And the fourth column, predictably, produced ratings that ranged from diplomatic to painfully honest.

The gaps in that whiteboard matrix told a story that months of engagement survey data had obscured rather than revealed, because engagement surveys, no matter how well-designed, measure what people are willing to say in a structured and observable format, not what is actually happening in the corridors, meeting rooms, and one-on-one conversations where culture is actually made. I have always held the view that if you need to rely on periodic staff attitude surveys to understand what your people think and what culture genuinely exists in your organisation, you are not communicating effectively with them throughout the year. Senior leaders who are genuinely connected to their culture know what the issues are on a daily basis and are proactively addressing them in real time, not waiting for the next survey cycle to confirm what the people closest to the work already know.

The whiteboard exercise gave the leadership team something the survey data had never provided: a structured and honest conversation about the architecture that would need to sit behind a healthy, successful, and sustainable culture. Not the aspiration of culture, but the machinery of it.

What culture actually is and is not

Culture is not a values statement. It is not an engagement score, a culture program, a team-building day, or an all-hands meeting where the CEO articulates the vision with genuine conviction. All of those things can be inputs to culture, but none of them is culture itself, and organisations that treat them as equivalent to culture are making an investment in the appearance of something they have not yet built.

Culture is the accumulated product of thousands of daily decisions made at every level of the organisation about what is acceptable and what is not, what is rewarded and what is ignored, what is modelled by leaders and what is tolerated despite being in contradiction to what those leaders say they stand for. It is built or degraded in the moment a leader decides whether to address an uncomfortable behavioural reality or allow it to pass unremarked. In the way a performance conversation is conducted or avoided. In whether the accountability standard that applies to a high performer is genuinely the same standard that applies to everyone else. In whether the organisation's tolerance for under-performance scales with the person's seniority, relationships, or commercial value.

What this means practically is that culture cannot be managed through communication, programs, or structural design alone. It requires all three elements working in concert and reinforced by consistent, visible, daily leadership behaviour at every level of the organisation. The moment the behaviour of leaders diverges from the culture the organisation claims to have, the culture the organisation *actually has* begins to be defined by that divergence. And the further down the organisation you go, the more clearly that divergence is visible to the people most affected by it.

The five conditions of a genuinely high-performance culture

There are five conditions that need to be simultaneously true for a culture to consistently produce the performance outcomes the organisation needs.

1. Values that are architecturally integrated, not decoratively displayed

The most powerful cultural system I have operated within was built on a philosophy that articulated, with remarkable clarity, exactly what the culture was designed to produce and how: *we select the right people, know the purpose of their role, measure the achievement of that purpose, incentivise that measurement, and recognise the achievement.* That is not a values statement. It is an operational architecture. Every element of it connects directly to a specific system, process, or practice that makes the philosophy visible in daily work: in the recruitment process; in how roles are defined; in how performance is measured and reported; in how compensation is structured; and in how recognition is delivered.

The test of whether your values are architecturally integrated or merely decoratively displayed is exactly the whiteboard exercise I described above. If you cannot complete column three; if the values cannot be measured or monitored then they are simply decoration.

2. A performance framework that harnesses core human motivation

One of the most consistent errors in how organisations design their performance and reward systems is the conflation of what people are paid and what actually motivates them. Compensation matters, but it is a hygiene factor rather than a motivator at the level required to produce genuinely discretionary effort and sustained high performance. What actually motivates people at work is a more fundamental set of human needs: the need for challenge and growth; for genuine recognition from people they respect; for a sense of ownership and agency over their own results; for a clear and visible connection between their individual effort and their individual outcome; and for the experience of belonging to something that has meaning and standards worth maintaining.

The travel organisation I described earlier understood this with unusual sophistication. Its performance framework, which included incentive-based compensation at every level from front-line through to executive, monthly performance conversations focused on recognition and forward action rather than retrospective assessment, highly visible recognition systems at daily, monthly and annual cadences, was designed explicitly around these human motivators rather than around the administrative convenience of the organisation. The result was a culture in which people at every level understood clearly what was expected. They could see in real time how they were performing against it, and had genuine financial and psychological incentive to close any gap.

3. Leadership consistency: the non-negotiable daily practice
Culture is not what leaders say. It is what leaders do, and more specifically what they do consistently under pressure when saying one thing and doing another would be easier. The visible behaviours that made the culture I am describing genuinely distinctive were not accidental or occasional. They were structural and consistent.

No private offices (including for the CEO) sent a daily signal that egalitarianism was operational and real, not aspirational. Monthly one-on-one conversations between every team leader and every team member were conducted to a consistent agenda, creating a rhythm of real engagement that meant issues surfaced continuously rather than accumulating to the point of crisis. Leaders at every level were expected to walk the talk visibly, specifically, and daily – not as a performance of cultural values but as the actual practice of them. Common sense over conventional wisdom was an explicit and empowering principle that gave people at every level permission to question and challenge the status quo rather than defer to hierarchy.

What I observed consistently in that culture, and have sought to replicate in different forms in every subsequent leadership role, is that the specific content of these practices mattered less than their consistency and their visibility.

People do not observe the values statement on the wall. They observe whether their leader's behaviour is consistent with it. The ten seconds a winner spent on stage at a global recognition event drove twelve months of performance not because of the ten seconds but because of everything it signalled about what the culture genuinely valued and was prepared to publicly affirm.

4. A structural architecture that enables rather than undermines the culture

The families, villages, tribes philosophy which was drawn from anthropological research on the strength and loyalty produced by small, stable social units, produced a structural design decision with profound cultural consequences: maximum teams of eight, everyone sitting together with no private offices, and performance reviews conducted within the team unit by the person who led that unit and worked alongside them daily, rather than by an HR department that was structurally distant from the work.

This was not a cultural initiative. It was an organisational design decision, and its cultural effect was substantial. It created the conditions for genuine accountability to people whose opinion mattered to each individual, rather than accountability to a system that was experienced as external and impersonal. The cultural implications of structural decisions; who sits next to whom, how teams are composed and sized, who conducts performance conversations and on what cadence, how information flows through the organisation, are consistently under-estimated in how organisations approach culture design.

Structure is not neutral with respect to culture. It either reinforces the culture you are trying to build or quietly works against it every single day.

5. Culture and strategy are explicitly connected and mutually accountable

The most common and costly cultural failure I encounter in organisations is the disconnect between the culture that leadership describes and the strategy the organisation is trying to execute. A culture that prioritises stability and consensus in an organisation whose strategy requires rapid adaptation and decisive risk-taking is not merely imperfect; it is actively preventing the strategy from being delivered.

A culture that rewards individual performance in isolation in an organisation whose strategy requires deep cross-functional collaboration is creating structural opposition to its own strategic objectives.

The test is specific: can you draw a direct and explicit line from each element of your stated culture to the strategic objectives it is designed to support, and then from those strategic objectives to the specific behaviours, systems, and practices that make the connection operational? If that line cannot be drawn, the culture and the strategy are operating in parallel rather than in concert, and the friction between them will be visible in the gap between what the strategy intends and what the organisation delivers.

Case Study: a retail lesson in performance architecture

In a COO role I held at a publicly listed retail business, I encountered one of the most instructive examples of the gap between what an incentive and performance system intends and what it actually produces, and of what happens when you redesign that system around the principles I have described throughout this book.

The existing incentive program was not unusual. It had for over 30 years been rewarding and focusing on a single metric at any given time, alternating between sales and margin.

The incentive mechanism rewarded people in a way that benefited predominantly the highest performing sellers, leaving the majority of the team in a structure that offered limited motivation for consistent improvement and no meaningful connection between their daily behaviour and the commercial outcomes the business needed. The program had accumulated variations and exceptions over time, producing a structure so complex that the people it was designed to motivate could not reliably calculate what they were working toward. In fact, after joining the business it took me over three weeks to find anyone in either head office or at store level who could even clearly articulate how the scheme worked. We discovered that less than five percent of the sales team were currently earning any bonus at all based on their sales performance and for those who did, it appeared to always come as a surprise to them.

In practical reality, it was effectively a dis-incentivisation scheme dressed as an incentive program.

What we built to replace it was grounded in exactly the cultural and performance architecture principles I have described in the preceding chapters. The new retail incentive program replaced all existing schemes with a single, unified structure built on a balanced scorecard approach; not just sales in isolation, but the full set of business drivers that actually determined store profitability: gross profit dollars (which balanced their approach to sales and margin) and percentage, conversion rates, attachment rates, cost management, and margin discipline.

Every metric was visible in real time through a purpose-built dashboard that every team member could access daily. Not a monthly report or a quarterly review, but a live and specific picture of exactly where they stood and what they needed to do to improve their position. More importantly, they could use it when negotiating price with a customer to show them exactly how much sales commission they were giving up by discounting.

The architecture had five elements that reflected the human motivation principles established earlier in this chapter.

A qualifying threshold ensured that the program rewarded genuine performance rather than participation. An accumulating tier structure meant that improvement at every level of performance generated additional incentive, not just improvement by the top performers. An acceleration and deceleration mechanism tied to margin percentage meant that the behaviours the business needed, specifically; disciplined pricing, quality selling and margin protection- were directly and visibly connected to individual financial outcomes.

A team-based overlay connected individual incentive to the overall store performance, creating genuine collective accountability rather than individual competition. And a store manager incentive pool with an uncapped accelerator tied to gross profit overachievement meant that the people with the most influence over team performance had the most direct and transparent stake in producing it.

Accompanying the incentive mechanism were the other critical elements of peer and company recognition – monetary rewards paid monthly and constant communication that featured the outstanding results of individuals and teams – which acted to drive further momentum.

The result was not incremental. The program delivered record profitability across the business, driven by a combination of performance improvement, genuine engagement at every level of the retail operation, and a quality of strategic alignment between individual behaviour and business outcome that had previously been structurally impossible.

Store managers who had previously focused predominantly on sales were now managing full P&L behaviours far more effectively with the right tools at their fingertips. Team members who had previously been outside the incentive structure were now active participants in the performance culture. And the daily use of the dashboard ensured that the morning meeting conversation was anchored in real data about yesterday's performance and today's opportunity, which created exactly the rhythm of continuous feedback and forward-focused coaching that the performance framework I described earlier as the engine of genuine capability development featured.

I want to draw attention to what this program would look like if it were being designed and implemented today with current AI capability available. The analytical architecture: the balanced scorecard, the tiered accumulation, the acceleration mechanics, and the team overlay would likely be identical, because those design principles are grounded in human motivation and organisational performance dynamics that AI does not change.

What AI would change today is the quality and timeliness of the insight available at every level of the system. The pattern recognition across stores, regions, and time periods that identifies the specific coaching intervention most likely to move a specific team member's performance. The predictive capability that flags a store whose margin trajectory suggests an incentive outcome problem two weeks before the month ends, when there is still time to address it. The analytical connection between individual behaviour patterns and store-level commercial outcomes at a level of specificity that previously required significant manual analysis and was therefore available only periodically rather than continuously.

The experience-intelligence edge in that retail context is not the AI capability alone and not the performance architecture alone. It is the combination: the human wisdom to design an incentive system that harnesses genuine human motivation, and the AI capability to make the feedback loops that drive it faster, more specific, and more continuously actionable than any manually operated system can sustain.

The Hewitt proof: what external validation actually means

I want to share something personal here about what the recognition I am about to describe actually meant to me, because understanding why it mattered is as important as the fact that it occurred.

During my tenure as global HR leader, we initiated what became a formal and ongoing pursuit of external best employer recognition through the Hewitt Best Employer program. Over the course of my tenure, including during the North American transformation described in earlier chapters, we achieved Best Employer recognition in four of our seven countries of operation.

We achieved Best Employer recognition in North America for each year of the transformation, which was a validation that the cultural architecture was real, not performative, even under genuine commercial pressure.

The conventional assumption, which I have heard articulated by leaders across many organisations, is that culture is a luxury of success. You can focus on building a genuinely great place to work when the commercial environment is stable and the transformation is complete, but during a crisis or a significant business reset, the culture work necessarily takes a back seat to the operational priorities that are more urgent.

The North American experience proved the opposite to be true, and proved it with external, independent validation. The proactive attention we gave to the structural cultural drivers and to the daily practice of the five conditions I have described above, maintained under genuine commercial pressure, was not a distraction from the commercial turnaround. It was a significant contributor to it.

Engaged people in a culture of genuine accountability, genuine recognition, and genuine leadership consistency produce better commercial outcomes than the same people in a culture of uncertainty, inconsistency, and unaddressed drift. That is not a philosophical position. It is an observable and measurable commercial reality.

The other point is this: we did not achieve external recognition through superior engagement survey scores. We achieved it because the structural drivers of genuine employer quality – the ones I have described throughout this chapter – were operational and consistent.

I have never believed that periodic staff surveys are an adequate or reliable mechanism for understanding the culture you actually have. If you need a formal survey to tell you what your people think and what issues exist in your culture, you are not sufficiently connected to the daily reality of your organisation to lead its culture effectively. The senior leaders who genuinely know their culture know it because they are in it daily: in the conversations, the team meetings, the one-on-ones, the recognition moments and the accountability conversations, and not because they review survey data quarterly and act on the themes. The survey can confirm what you already know if you are leading well. It should never be the primary mechanism through which you discover it.

The leader's role: what only YOU can do

Everything I have described in this chapter so far can be designed, structured, and resourced. The performance framework, the recognition architecture, the structural design, and the connection between culture and strategy. All of these are buildable with the right investment of deliberate leadership effort.

What cannot be built by design, resourced through investment, or delegated to a culture program is the daily, personal, consistent leadership behaviour that ultimately determines whether the architecture produces the culture it was designed to produce or gradually drifts into a more comfortable but less effective approximation of it.

There are specific and non-delegable leadership behaviours that hold a high-performance culture together, and they are worth naming plainly.

The first is **modelling the standard publicly and consistently**.

This happens not in the moments that are easy and visible but in the moments that are difficult and where the easier option is to look the other way. Every time a leader allows a behaviour that contradicts the stated culture to pass unremarked (or worse still, is the culprit themselves), they redefine the culture more powerfully than any values statement can restore it. Every time they hold the line in a moment where it would be easier not to, they reinforce it more effectively than any culture program can achieve.

The second is **staying genuinely connected to the real day-to-day knowledge and experience of the organisation at every level**. Not through surveys or escalated issues, but through the daily disciplines of presence, conversation, and honest inquiry that keep the leader's picture of the culture current and accurate. The leaders I have observed build and sustain the most genuinely effective cultures share a distinctive characteristic: they know what is actually happening in their organisations because they have built the habits and the relationships that make that knowledge continuously available to them. They do not discover cultural issues in the annual survey. They surface and address them in real time.

The third is **resisting the drift toward comfort**: the gradual and almost invisible accommodation of lower standards that occurs in every organisation over time and that, left unaddressed, eventually produces the kind of cultural gap that the whiteboard exercise reveals. The most dangerous cultural moment in any high-performance organisation is not the dramatic failure or the visible crisis. It is the small, quiet accommodation, sometimes the standard that is not enforced just this once, the conversation that is deferred because the timing is difficult, the behaviour that is tolerated because the person exhibiting it is valuable in other ways. These moments accumulate, and their accumulation is the mechanism by which genuinely great cultures become merely adequate ones without anyone making a conscious decision that it should be so.

Culture and AI: the specific risk and the specific opportunity

The introduction of AI into an organisation's operating environment creates cultural consequences that most leadership teams are not yet thinking about with sufficient deliberateness, and those consequences cut in two directions.

The risk is specific: AI tools introduced without adequate leadership intentionality tend to accelerate the existing cultural dynamics of the organisation rather than improving them. In a culture of genuine accountability and disciplined performance management, AI amplifies the rigour and quality of that accountability. In a culture where accountability is inconsistent, where performance data is managed rather than acted on, and where the gap between stated standards and lived reality is already significant, AI generates better data about a problem the organisation does not yet have the cultural architecture to address. The data becomes evidence of the gap without providing the leadership conditions required to close it, and the result is often a sophisticated analytical capability sitting on top of an unchanged cultural reality, which is, in my observation, one of the most expensive and demoralising combinations available to a leadership team.

The opportunity is equally specific: when AI is introduced into an organisation that has already built the five conditions I have described: values with operational architecture, a performance framework connected to human motivation, consistent leadership behaviour, structural design that reinforces the culture, and explicit connection between culture and strategy, it can do things for cultural quality and consistency that were previously limited by human bandwidth.

It can surface the leading indicators of cultural drift before they become lagging indicators of cultural failure. It can make the connection between individual behaviour and organisational outcome visible at a level of specificity and timeliness that changes how people experience the relationship between their daily practice and the culture they are collectively producing. And it can support the leader's daily connection to the lived experience of the organisation in ways that extend rather than replace the human judgement and human relationship that remain at the core of genuine cultural leadership.

The principle I apply in my advisory work is simple. AI is a cultural accelerant, not a cultural solution. The direction in which it accelerates is determined by the quality of the cultural and human architecture it operates within.

What a high-performance culture feels like from the inside

I want to close the substantive argument of this chapter with something that culture frameworks and diagnostic tools rarely manage to convey: what it actually feels like to work inside a genuinely high-performance culture when it is operating at its best.

It feels like clarity. People at every level know what is expected of them, why it matters, and how their individual contribution connects to the outcome the organisation is trying to produce.

There is no ambiguity about the standard, and no uncertainty about whether the standard applies to them specifically.

It feels like genuine energy and it is hugely empowering. Not the performed enthusiasm of an organisation that has recently completed an imposed culture program, but the real and durable energy of people who are being genuinely challenged, recognised, and led by people whose behaviour they respect because it is consistent with what they say.

It feels like psychological safety of a specific kind, not the safety of an absence of accountability, but the safety of knowing that the rules are the same and consistently applied for everyone, that dissent is eagerly heard and encouraged rather than suppressed, and that the organisation's stated values will be defended rather than abandoned when defending them becomes inconvenient.

And it feels like momentum. The particular quality of collective forward motion that occurs when an organisation's culture and strategy are genuinely aligned and when the way people behave every day is actively supporting the direction in which the organisation is trying to move.

This felt experience of clarity, energy, and momentum is not just anecdotal. Reviews of hundreds of studies on team performance and psychological safety now converge on the same conclusion. Teams perform best when people can speak up without fear **and** when standards remain explicit and non-negotiable.

Or in Edmondson's language, the most effective cultures live in the learning zone: high psychological safety and high accountability at the same time and not in the comfort zone of low standards or the anxiety zone of fear-based pressure.

I have been inside cultures that produced that feeling, and I have worked hard to build it in organisations that did not.

It is not accidental, and it is not fragile once genuinely built. But it requires the architecture, the consistency, and the daily leadership discipline that this chapter has attempted to describe. Most importantly, it requires a leader who understands that culture is not something the organisation has. It is something the leader produces, daily, through every decision about what to model, what to reward, and what to hold the line on when holding the line is the harder choice.

TOOLBOX — Chapter 11

Questions to build and sustain a high-performance culture

A. Questions on cultural architecture

1. If we did the whiteboard exercise right now; listing each stated value, what behaviour it requires, how that behaviour is monitored, and how consistently it is modelled, what would the gaps tell us about the real culture of this organisation versus the one we describe?

2. Which of our stated values has a direct and traceable connection to a specific system, process, or leadership practice that makes it operational, and which exist only in the statement?

3. Where in this organisation are the most significant gaps between what the culture says it stands for and what it demonstrably permits, and what has prevented those gaps from being addressed?

4. How would a new employee with no prior knowledge of our culture describe it after ninety days, based purely on what they observed rather than what they were told?

5. What is the single behaviour that, if it changed tomorrow at the most senior level, would do more to shift the culture than any program or initiative currently underway?

B. Questions on performance, recognition and reward

1. Does our performance and reward framework create a direct and visible connection between individual effort and individual outcome at every level of the organisation or does it

reward tenure, seniority, or role rather than genuine contribution?

2. Are our recognition systems designed around core human motivators; challenge, genuine acknowledgement, ownership, belonging, and visible progress or around administrative convenience?

3. What behaviours do our current incentive and recognition architecture reward that we would not endorse if we examined them explicitly, and what does that tell us about what our culture is actually measuring?

4. How frequently and in what format does every person in this organisation receive a genuine, specific, and forward-focused performance conversation from their direct leader and is that frequency and quality consistent across all levels and functions?

5. Where in this organisation is the gap between the performance of the highest and lowest contributors being tolerated in a way that signals to everyone that the performance standard is aspirational rather than operational?

C. Questions on leadership consistency

1. In the last thirty days, what specific behaviours have I modelled that were consistent with the culture I am trying to build and what behaviours have I exhibited or permitted that were inconsistent with it?

2. Where in this organisation are the leaders whose behaviour most diverges from the stated culture and what is the consequence, if any, of that divergence?

3. How do I stay genuinely connected to the lived experience of the organisation at every level; not through survey data or escalated issues but through the daily habits of presence, conversation, and honest inquiry?

4. What is the last uncomfortable cultural conversation I avoided or deferred and what signal did that avoidance send to the people who observed it?

5. If the people who work for me described my leadership behaviour to a new team member, how close would that description be to the culture I say I am trying to build?

D. Questions on culture and strategy alignment

1. Can I draw a direct and explicit line from each element of our stated culture to the specific strategic objectives it is designed to support?

2. Where in this organisation is the culture actively working against the strategy; producing friction, slowing adaptation, or rewarding behaviours that are inconsistent with the direction in which we need to move?

3. What does our current culture make easy that our strategy requires to be easy and what does it make difficult that our strategy requires to be straightforward?

4. How explicitly has the leadership team discussed the specific cultural conditions required for the current strategy to succeed and where are those conditions absent?

5. In twelve months, what would the culture of this organisation need to look like for the strategy we are currently executing to have produced its intended outcomes?

E. Questions on AI and culture

1. Are we introducing AI into an organisation whose cultural architecture is strong enough to use it well, or into a culture where it will accelerate existing problems rather than address them?

2. What cultural consequences has the introduction of AI tools already produced in this organisation that we have not yet discussed explicitly?

3. Where are AI-generated insights about performance, behaviour, or outcomes sitting in the organisation without being acted on and what does that tell us about the cultural conditions required to translate analytical capability into changed behaviour?

4. How are we ensuring that the efficiency and scale AI provides to our performance management does not come at the cost of the human relationship and human judgement that genuine cultural leadership requires?

5. What would our culture need to look like in three years for AI to be contributing to it at the level of its genuine potential, and what do we need to build now to make that possible?

Closing Reflection — Chapter 11

The manufacturing leadership team that sat in front of that whiteboard and saw the gaps had not built a poor culture through indifference or bad intentions. They had built it through the entirely normal accumulation of small accommodations, deferred conversations, and unmeasured aspirations that produces, in almost every organisation that does not deliberately and consistently defend against it, the gap between the culture described and the culture lived.

Closing that gap is not a program. It is not a values refresh or an engagement survey or a culture workshop, though all of those can play a role in a broader architecture that is genuinely committed to the work. It is the daily practice of holding the line: of measuring what you say you value, of modelling the standard you expect of others, of building the structural conditions that make high performance the natural default rather than the exceptional achievement, and of staying genuinely connected to the lived reality of the organisation you are leading rather than the one you would prefer to believe you have.

That is both the weight and the privilege of the leader's role in culture. And there is no version of it that can be outsourced, automated, or avoided. Culture is where the Discipline Dividend is most visible and most felt: not in a framework or an engagement score, but in the daily lived experience of an organisation whose leader has held the line, day after day, in the moments where looking the other way would have been easier. The organisations I have seen build this do not describe it as discipline. They describe it as the way we do things here. That description, when it is genuinely true, is the dividend.

Here is a space for your own reflection on this chapter. What resonated with you?

(Write your thoughts here)

____

____

____

____

____

____

CHAPTER 12

THE EXPERIENCE-INTELLIGENCE EDGE: WHERE HUMAN WISDOM MEETS ARTIFICIAL INTELLIGENCE

"Imagination is more important than knowledge. For knowledge is limited, whereas imagination embraces the entire world."

—Albert Einstein,
Theoretical Physicist

Experience tells you what matters. AI intelligence scales what you know. Together, they are unstoppable.

There is a conversation I find myself having with increasing frequency in my advisory work, and it tends to follow a recognisable pattern.

A leadership team has decided to invest in AI. They have identified the tools, secured the budget, and briefed the organisation on the transformation ahead. What they have not done (which becomes immediately apparent) is ask the question that determines whether the investment produces genuine organisational capability or an expensive and demoralising approximation of it: what specific human wisdom needs to sit alongside this technology for it to do what we are expecting it to do?

The question matters because AI, applied without the experiential judgement to direct it, contextualise it, and hold it accountable for the quality of its outputs, is not a capability accelerant. It is an efficiency tool at best and a sophisticated distraction at worst. The organisations that are genuinely extracting transformational value from AI are not the ones with the most advanced tools or the largest implementation budgets. They are the ones where experienced leaders understand both what AI can see that humans cannot, and what humans must contribute that AI cannot replicate, and have built the operating architecture that brings those two capabilities into genuine partnership.

That intersection; what I call the experience-intelligence edge, is what this final chapter is about. And the argument I want to make is a personal one, because it is grounded in a career spent building exactly the kind of human capability and organisational wisdom that AI now has the power to extend in ways that were not previously available.

The question is not whether to use AI. That question has already been answered by the pace of its adoption across every sector and every organisational scale. The question is what kind of leader you need to be to use it well, and what that combination of human experience and artificial intelligence makes possible that neither can produce alone.

What experience provides that AI cannot

Across the chapters of this book, I have described a set of capabilities that I have built, applied, and refined across a career spanning multiple sectors, geographies, and degrees of organisational complexity and commercial pressure.

Specifically, the accountability reset architecture, the Root Cause Diagnostic Framework, the capability development conditions, the commercial L&D model, the decision-making framework, the communication architecture and the five conditions of a high-performance culture.

These are not theoretical frameworks. They are the distilled product of direct, consequential experience and of building things that worked, making decisions that did not, and developing through both the judgement required to tell the difference in real time under genuine pressure for results and outcomes.

What experience provides, and what AI in its current form cannot replicate, is the capacity to make that kind of judgement in conditions of genuine ambiguity: where the data is incomplete; the stakeholders are complex; the organisational context is specific in ways that no training dataset fully captures; and the consequences of being wrong affect real people.

As we have discussed, AI is extraordinarily capable at pattern recognition across large datasets, at generating options and stress-testing assumptions, at surfacing the analytical insights that human cognitive bandwidth cannot process at the same scale or speed.

However, just as it is impossible to take any business book at face value and expect it to deliver the same results without appropriate contextualisation for your own situation, neither can AI-generated knowledge assist you with many aspects of leadership that rely on human nuances.

AI cannot sit across a table from a leadership team that is frightened, or resistant, or operating in bad faith, and know from decades of having done exactly that, what the conversation actually requires. Sometimes that is challenge, sometimes reassurance, sometimes the willingness to name something that everyone in the room is aware of and nobody has yet said aloud.

The experience-intelligence edge is the product of those two capabilities working seamlessly together. The analytical reach and pattern recognition of AI directed and contextualised by the human judgement that knows which patterns and application of knowledge matter in this specific situation, for this specific organisation, at this specific moment in its history. And more valuably, has the leadership ability to recognise and manage human behaviours in real-time and in practice, that AI does not.

You saw one version of this in contemplation of how AI could have super-charged the retail incentive program we spoke to in the previous chapter; a balanced scorecard architecture built on human motivation, then amplified by live data and disciplined feedback loops.

If that same program were being built today, AI would not replace the human design work or practical insights into the triggers for empowering and amplifying human sales behaviour in the organisational context within which the model was constructed. It would make the pattern recognition, prediction and coaching insight faster and more precise. That is the experience-intelligence edge in practice that is at our finger-tips today with AI enhancement.

What to do from here

This book has been, from its opening pages, an argument about the gap between the leadership that organisations say they want and the leadership architecture required to produce it consistently. The accountability that is talked about but not built or embedded systemically in the organisation. The capability development that is funded but not connected to the work or outcomes that actually demand it. The decision-making discipline that is endorsed in the abstract but abandoned under the pressure of urgency, hierarchy, and the entirely human preference for comfortable answers. The culture that is described with genuine conviction by leaders who have not examined the gap between the description and the daily reality with the rigour that closing it requires.

The argument has been practical and hopefully pragmatic throughout, because the gap is practical. It is not closed by better intention or more compelling vision. It is closed by the architectural decisions about systems, processes, measurement, leadership behaviour, and the consistent daily practice of holding the line that make the organisation's stated standards operational rather than aspirational.

AI does not change that argument. It extends it. It makes the measurement more precise, the feedback loops faster, the pattern recognition across complex organisational data more powerful than human bandwidth alone can sustain. But the architecture it operates within, which is the human judgement, the leadership consistency, the cultural conditions, the decision discipline, all remain the determinant of whether it produces genuine organisational capability or merely a more sophisticated picture of an unchanged reality.

The leaders who will use AI most effectively in the decade ahead are not primarily those with the deepest technical fluency. They are those with the deepest understanding of what organisations actually require to perform, and the wisdom to direct AI's analytical power toward the problems that most need solving and the opportunities that most deserve pursuing.

That powerful combination of experience and intelligence, human wisdom and artificial capability, the lessons of the past and the analytical reach of the future, is the edge that is genuinely available to every leader who is willing to build it. And building it starts not with the technology but with the clarity about what you are trying to produce, the honesty about what is currently preventing it, and the architectural discipline to close the gap between the two.

That is, and has always been, the work.

The architecture in summary: what eleven chapters built

If I were to compress the argument of this entire book into a single conversation, the kind I might have with a senior leader who had two hours and a genuine willingness to be honest about what was and wasn't working in their organisation, it would move through five specific questions in sequence.

The first: *Where has discipline and accountability become optional?*

Not in the stated values or the aspirational frameworks, but in the daily reality of what this organisation consistently tolerates and rewards with respect to performance and outcomes. That gap between the accountability the organisation describes and the accountability it actually enforces, is where the Discipline Dividend either begins to compound or begins to erode.

The second: *Is the capability architecture connected to the required work?*

Not to the programs, the modules, or the satisfaction scores but to the specific strategic challenges the organisation needs its people to be able to solve, under the four conditions that produce genuine growth: real challenge; real accountability; honest feedback close to the work; and the expressed belief of a leader who is genuinely invested in someone's development rather than simply responsible for it.

The third: *What is the quality of the decisions being made, and what is the decision architecture producing them?*

Smart people in poorly designed decision environments make poor decisions with genuine confidence. The question is not whether the leaders are capable. It is whether the environment they operate within is deliberately designed to highlight what they don't know, challenge what they believe, and hold the assumptions on which their decisions rest to a standard of evidence rather than narrative.

The fourth: *What does the culture actually permit?*

Not what the values statement says. What the organisation demonstrably tolerates when holding the line is inconvenient, what it rewards when the reward conflicts with the stated standard, and what it models when the leaders who are supposed to embody it are under pressure.

The fifth, and the question this final chapter has been built around: *What role is AI playing in each of these domains and is it accelerating the architecture or substituting for it?*

The answer to that question will, in my view, be one of the defining competitive differentiators of the next decade. Not because AI is the most important element of the equation, but because its presence makes the quality of the architecture it operates within more visible, more consequential, and harder to paper over than it has ever been before.

These five questions are not a framework in the conventional sense. They are the shape of an honest conversation; the kind that the organisations I have described in this book, at their best moments, were prepared to have with themselves and continue to explore. And the organisations I have seen struggle were, almost without exception, the ones that found reasons to defer it.

The Discipline Dividend is not a destination. It is a practice and like all practices worth maintaining, it requires a decision to start, and a daily decision to continue. The most important question this book can leave you with is not conceptual. It is personal. Where, specifically, in your organisation be that in your team, your board or your daily leadership habits, is discipline currently optional when it should be architectural?

That is where the work begins. And the compounding benefits start the moment you choose to do it.

Closing Reflection — Chapter 12

I began this book with the observation that the organisations most frustrated by their leadership gaps are almost always the same ones whose approach to closing those gaps is most disconnected from the reality of what closing them requires.

That observation points toward the same conclusion in every domain I have explored: accountability, capability, decision architecture, culture, and now the integration of human experience with artificial intelligence. The gap is almost never closed by good intentions, compelling vision, or the investment in programs and tools that address the symptoms rather than the architecture. It is closed by discipline that is specific, consistent, architecturally embedded, and maintained without exception in the daily practice of every leader at every level of the organisation.

The Discipline Dividend is this book's central argument, stated plainly again now at its close:

> *Organisations and leaders that apply discipline consistently, that build clear expectations, hold the accountability line, develop capability rigorously,*

make decisions with genuine architectural rigour, and defend their cultural standards in the moments when defence is hardest, earn compound returns in performance, confidence, and commercial outcomes that are invisible in the short term and transformational over time.

Like all compounding, the returns are not available to leaders who apply discipline selectively, or inconsistently, or until the pressure of competing priorities makes the comfortable alternative feel justified. They are available only to those who hold the line through the accountability conversation that needs to happen this week, in the cultural standard that needs to be defended this month, in the decision process that needs to be completed properly this quarter, and who understand that every time they do, they are not simply managing an organisation. They are building one.

That is the work. It has always been the work. The tools available to do it have never been more powerful. The organisations that use those tools in the service of genuine architectural discipline, rather than as a substitute for it, will earn returns that compound for as long as they choose to hold the line.

The Discipline Dividend is available to every leader who is willing to build it. The only question is when you start.

I hope this book has given you the practical tools and confidence to start on that journey today!

USING THE PLAYBOOKS IN PRACTICE

The three-stage pattern that runs through this book: Drift, Discipline, and Dividend, is most useful when you apply it as a diagnostic lens to your own organisation before you begin.

Where are standards softening? Where has accountability become optional or inconsistent? And where is discipline already producing a compounding return that you can build on? Your honest answers to those three questions will tell you where to start.

As is always the case, the value of this book will not come from agreeing or empathising with it while sipping a cappuccino (no matter how comforting that may be!).

It will come from what you actually choose to do with it next and I really hope you will take action where it will make the biggest difference in your life.

The playbooks and toolboxes throughout these chapters are designed to help you move from diagnosis to disciplined action in a way that fits your own unique context, your role, and the realities of the organisation you are working in.

You do not need to implement everything at once. In fact, trying to do that will usually create a lot more noise than progress. The better approach is to start where the cost of drift is currently highest. For some leaders, that will be accountability: the conversations being avoided, the standards that have become negotiable, and the uneven follow-through that is quietly exhausting capable people.

For others, it will be judgement and decision-making: where there is simply too much complexity, too little thinking support when it comes down to the "crunch", and too many important decisions carried in isolation.

For others still, the starting point will be culture and capability: where leadership action is not properly aligned to the aspired values and where work needs to be done to rebuild the conditions in which people can perform well without burning themselves out.

A practical way to use this book is to choose one priority domain first. If accountability is your pressure point, begin with Chapters 5 and 8 and work through the accompanying toolboxes with your leadership team.

If decision quality is the bigger issue, start with Chapters 6, 7, 10, and 12, and use those frameworks to examine how judgement is currently supported, challenged, and translated into action.

If culture, confidence, and sustainable performance are the concern, Chapters 3, 4, 9, and 11 provide the strongest foundation for that work.

Another useful approach is to apply the material over a ninety-day period. Use the first thirty days to diagnose honestly: where standards are unclear, where accountability is unsupported, where decisions are heavier than they should be, and where culture is relying too much on heroic individuals rather than disciplined systems.

Use the next thirty days to reset one or two structural practices: clarify expectations, tighten a decision process, redesign a leadership conversation, or introduce one new rhythm of review and follow-through. Use the final thirty days to assess what is changing, what resistance has surfaced, and what still needs to be reinforced before the gains begin to compound.

These playbooks are not intended to be theoretical ideals. They are meant to be used in boardrooms, executive and leadership meetings, one-on-ones, strategy sessions, off-sites, and the quiet moments of reflection where leaders decide whether they are prepared to hold the line with greater consistency than before. The aim is definitely not perfection. The aim is to build disciplined architecture that makes better performance, clearer judgement, continual improvement and healthier cultures more likely by design.

Where AI is concerned, the same principle applies. Use it to sharpen your thinking, test assumptions, challenge incomplete reasoning, and increase the quality of preparation. Do not use it as a substitute for judgement, courage, or accountability. Those remain deeply human responsibilities and skills that I believe will become far more valuable in coming years.

What AI can do, if approached well, is make disciplined leadership easier to support, easier to scale, and harder to fake.

If you are unsure where to begin, begin where the friction (and often cynicism) is greatest. Start with the recurring issue that your organisation explains away, casually refers to often, revisits repeatedly, or quietly tolerates because addressing it properly feels inconvenient, political, or uncomfortable. That is often where the absence of discipline is costing you the most, and where rebuilding it will create the greatest dividend.

To all the leaders fighting the good fight of discipline
and accountability — stay strong. The dividend is real,
and it is worth every uncomfortable conversation.

CONTINUE THE WORK

The Discipline Dividend was never intended to be a set of ideas you put back on the shelf. It is an operating architecture and its value is only realised when the knowledge is applied, tested, and refined in the real conditions and operating context of your organisation.

If you are ready to continue the work beyond these pages, there are several ways we can do that together.

Leadership Programs: The Discipline Dividend in practice

The Discipline Dividend Leadership Program translates the frameworks in this book into a structured development journey for leaders and teams. Through a combination of self-paced learning, practical tools, real-work application tasks, and optional cohort-based experiences, the program is designed to help you:

- Diagnose where discipline is currently optional in your organisation.
- Reset accountability and decision architecture in ways that hold under pressure.
- Build the cultural and capability conditions that make high performance sustainable.

Details of current program offerings including governance learning are available at:

Website: www.andreaslingsby.com

Speaking, board advisory, and executive sessions

For leadership teams and boards who want to engage with these ideas in a concentrated format, I speak and facilitate sessions on topics including:

- The Discipline Dividend: why some organisations compound and others quietly erode.
- Accountability without the landmines.
- Decision-making under pressure: closing the judgement gap.
- Culture as architecture, not aspiration.
- The experience–intelligence edge: governing and leading in an AI-enabled world.

These sessions can be delivered in person or virtually, and are often used to anchor a board off-site, executive retreat, or the launch of an internal leadership program.

For enquiries about speaking, board advisory work, or bespoke executive sessions, please reach out through www.andreaslingsby.com

The compound returns are always larger when you have resources to tap into.

However you choose to continue the work, the principle remains the same: every time you hold the line on accountability, decision quality, capability, and culture, you are not simply managing an organisation.

You are building one.
All the best!

Warmest regards
Andrea

REFERENCES AND NOTES

Introduction

1. Clear, J. (2018). *Atomic Habits: An easy and proven way to build good habits and break bad ones.* Avery/Penguin Random House.

Chapter 4: Why Good Leaders Stopped Holding the Line

2. McCall, M. W., & Lombardo, M. M. (1983). *Off the track: Why and how successful executives get derailed* (Technical Report No. 21). Center for Creative Leadership.
3. Lombardo, M. M., & McCauley, C. D. (1988). *The dynamics of management derailment* (Technical Report No. 34). Center for Creative Leadership.
4. United States Department of Justice. (2020, February 21). *Wells Fargo agrees to pay $3 billion to resolve criminal and civil investigations into sales practices involving the opening of millions of accounts without customer authorization* [Press release]. Office of Public Affairs.
5. Tayan, B. (2019). *The Wells Fargo cross-selling scandal.* Harvard Law School Forum on Corporate Governance.

Chapter 4: Psychological Safety and Performance

6. Edmondson, A. C. (1999). Psychological safety and learning behavior in work teams. *Administrative Science Quarterly, 44*(2), 350–383.

7.   Edmondson, A. C. (2018). *The fearless organization: Creating psychological safety in the workplace for learning, innovation, and growth.* John Wiley & Sons.

8.   Brooks, A. C. (2022). *From strength to strength: Finding success, happiness, and deep purpose in the second half of life.* Portfolio/Penguin.

Chapter 5: Accountability Without the Landmines

9.   *Work Health and Safety Amendment (Managing Psychosocial Hazards) Regulation 2022* (Cth). Safe Work Australia.

10.   *Health and Safety at Work etc. Act 1974* (UK). Health and Safety Executive.

11.   *Management of Health and Safety at Work Regulations 1999* (UK). Health and Safety Executive.

12.   Mental Health Commission of Canada. (2013). *National standard of Canada for psychological health and safety in the workplace* (CAN/CSA-Z1003-13/BNQ 9700-803/2013). CSA Group.

13.   Council of the European Union. (1989). *Council Directive 89/391/EEC of 12 June 1989 on the introduction of measures to encourage improvements in the safety and health of workers at work* (EU Framework Directive). *Official Journal of the European Communities.*

14.   United States Occupational Safety and Health Administration. (1970). *General Duty Clause, Section 5(a)(1) of the Occupational Safety and Health Act of 1970*, 29 U.S.C. § 654(a)(1).

15.   Comcare. (2025, December 18). *Defence convicted after RAAF worker's death* [Media release].

16.   *Commonwealth Work Health and Safety Act 2011* (Cth), ss. 19(1), 33.

17.   *Comcare v Department of Defence* (NSW Local Court, Newcastle, 19 December 2025, Magistrate Brett Thomas).

18.   Bazigos, M., Gagnon, C., & Schaninger, B. (2016, April). Leadership in context. *McKinsey Quarterly.*

Chapter 6: The Judgement Gap — Why Decisions Are Getting Worse

19. Janis, I. L. (1982). *Groupthink: Psychological studies of policy decisions and fiascoes* (2nd ed.). Houghton Mifflin.
20. Sunstein, C. R., & Hastie, R. (2015). *Wiser: Getting beyond groupthink to make groups smarter.* Harvard Business Review Press.
21. Kahneman, D. (2011). *Thinking, fast and slow.* Farrar, Straus and Giroux.
22. Heath, C., & Heath, D. (2013). *Decisive: How to make better choices in life and work.* Crown Business.
23. Australian Institute of Company Directors. (2024). *AICD director sentiment index.*
24. Australian Institute of Company Directors. (2019). *Good governance principles and guidance for not-for-profit organisations.*
25. Kiel, G., Nicholson, G., Tunny, J. A., & Beck, J. (2012). *Directors at work: A practical guide for boards.* Thomson Reuters Australia.

Chapter 8: The Accountability Playbook: Rebuilding the Line After It Has Been Lost

26. *Comcare v Department of Defence* (NSW Local Court, Newcastle, 19 December 2025, Magistrate Brett Thomas).
27. Comcare. (2025, December 18). *Defence convicted after RAAF worker's death.*
28. Commonwealth of Australia. (2011). *Work Health and Safety Act 2011 (Cth)*, ss. 19(1), 33.

Chapter 9: Growing People at the Speed Organisations Actually Need

29. Lombardo, M. M., & Eichinger, R. W. (1996). *The career architect development planner* (1st ed.). Lominger Limited.
30. McCall, M. W., Lombardo, M. M., & Morrison, A. M. (1988). *The lessons of experience: How successful executives develop on the job.* Lexington Books/Free Press.

Chapters 10 and 11: Decision-Making and Organisational Design

31. Kahneman, D. (2011). *Thinking, fast and slow.* Farrar, Straus and Giroux.
32. Heath, C., & Heath, D. (2013). *Decisive: How to make better choices in life and work.* Crown Business.
33. Nicholson, N. (2000). *Managing the human animal.* Texere Publishing. (Published in the United States as *The executive instinct.*)
34. Nicholson, N. (1997). Evolutionary psychology: Toward a new view of human nature and organizational society. *Human Relations, 50*(9), 1053–1078.
35. Nicholson, N. (1998). How hardwired is human behavior? *Harvard Business Review, 76*(4), 134–147.

www.ingramcontent.com/pod-product-compliance
Lightning Source LLC
Chambersburg PA
CBHW071304140726
47996CB00005B/1620